DAKOTA EPIC

◆

HATZELL
1989

Stefan's
SKETCHES

WOLVES

USED ON LOCATION FOR THE FILM
" DANCES WITH WOLVES"

RENDERED MONDAY AFTERNOON
AUGUST 21, 1989

DAKOTA EPIC

◆

Experiences of a Reenactor During the Filming of *Dances With Wolves*

Bill Markley with illustrations by Jim Hatzell

Writer's Showcase
San Jose New York Lincoln Shanghai

DAKOTA EPIC
Experiences of a Reenactor During the Filming of *Dances With Wolves*

Writer's Showcase
an imprint of iUniverse.com, Inc.

For information address:
iUniverse.com, Inc.
5220 S 16th, Ste. 200
Lincoln, NE 68512
www.iuniverse.com

ISBN: 0-595-19521-0

Printed in the United States of America

This book is dedicated to everyone who has been in the background of a movie and to all those who have been cut out of a scene.

We thought we knowed it all, but it didn't take long ter find out 't we didn't know nothin'.

—Wilbur F. Hinman, *Corporal Si Klegg and His Pard*

Contents

◆

List of Illustrations

◆

Foreword

◆

Bill Markley is an excellent tour guide to the world of movie-making. I know this because he made an empty field come alive for me with the sounds of the Civil War. Several years ago he gave members of the Kevin Costner Fan Club a tour of the site used for the battle scene in *Dances With Wolves*. As Bill talked to us, I could almost see Lieutenant Dunbar galloping across the uneven ground, daring the Confederate soldiers to shoot him (Bill was one of those soldiers). That field didn't look nearly so dangerous in the movie! I marveled that Kevin could ride a horse across the uneven ground, at full gallop and without holding the reins. Seeing the movie through Bill's eyes was the next best thing to visiting the set itself.

The magic of movie-making has long fascinated the American public. Yet few of us get a glimpse of what it is really like. Being an extra in a movie—one of the people seen in the background—is a privilege that few of us have. Bill Markley had that privilege, and not in just any movie, but in one of the best movies ever made. *Dances With Wolves* won seven Academy Awards and was named one of the 100 best films of the 20th century. What was it like to be part of this epic? To watch the tapestry of the story being woven each day, to be part of the work and the laughter and yes, the frustration that goes into the making of a movie—that is a magic in itself!

We are lucky that Bill kept a journal during his time as an extra. We are even luckier that he has decided to share it with us. Come along for a fascinating journey into Kevin Costner's frontier world!

Cindy Northup
Vice-President,
The Kevin Costner International Fan Club
February 23, 2001

Preface

◆

During the filming of *Dances With Wolves* in South Dakota, I had the good fortune to be selected as a reenactor extra for the Civil War, Ft. Hays, and pursuit of Dunbar sets. During these time periods, I kept a detailed journal on what it was like to be a part of the filming. Jim Hatzell, also a reenactor extra and an artist from Rapid City, South Dakota, drew quick sketches of life on the set. Jim and I have worked together to develop what we think is a unique view of life on a film set from the extra's point of view.

This book is based on my journal written during the filming of *Dances With Wolves*. Some of those who were involved in the filming have reviewed it for accuracy. Anyone who keeps a journal knows when the action is hot and heavy it gets harder to find the time and energy to write. This is my perspective of the making of *Dances With Wolves*—if you will, from a microscopic viewpoint as opposed to someone in charge who would have a macroscopic view. Jim Hatzell's illustrations are taken from his on-scene quick sketches.

Acknowledgements

◆

First, all thanks belong to my Lord and Savior Jesus Christ. It *is* a wonderful life! I thank Liz, my wife for telling me to go for it. I thank my parents for their enthusiasm for all my adventures. I thank my kids, Becky and Chris, for being the greatest in the world. Special thanks to Kevin Costner and the entire film crew for putting together a truly epic motion picture and for allowing reenactors to participate and at times make suggestions. Thank you Jim Wilson, Megaly Doty, and Beth Kirkpatrick with Tig Productions for the manuscript review and giving the go-ahead from Tig. Thanks to my pards, Bruce Huxford and Tim Larson for your help. Thanks to all the reenactors who helped lead a rookie through the beginnings of infantry and cavalry reenacting. I want to thank Terry Pool and my brother Doug for their review and moral support. Thanks to Gerry Barnes for his critical review and to Nancy Koupal for her assistance. Jim Borchers, thanks for your insight into the story-telling. Special thanks to Cindy Northup for her critique and assistance. Jim Hatzell, thanks man for the review and the great illustrations. Thanks Sheryl Torguson for dotting my i's and crossing my t's. Theta Bowden thanks bro. for picking at "merely nits." Ken and Linda Thompson, Grayson Bagley, and Tom Byron thanks for your enthusiastic encouragement. Rifka Keilson and the folks are iUniverse.com thank you for all your help. Thanks to Dennis Ryckman,

Bob Burke, and Sarah Bryan with My Tech Place, Inc. for scanning and embedding the images for this book. Whoever developed spell check for computers–thanks!

Introduction

◆

Dakota Epic is about making the film *Dances With Wolves* from an extra's viewpoint. I was a Civil War reenacting extra in the film's opening battlefield scenes, at Ft. Hays, and in the winter pursuit of Dunbar through Spearfish Canyon.

"What was it like to be in *Dances With Wolves*?" people ask.

"It was a great experience. One of the high points of my life!" I then quickly add "But not as great as getting married and having kids!"

This is an account of what it was like to be an extra on the set of *Dances With Wolves*. It is not a documentary about how movies are made. I am still not sure how everything is done to make a movie, or what most of the film industry terminology means. What is a grip or a gaffer anyway? This story does not concentrate on Kevin Costner or any of the other big name actors or movie industry people. They did not know me; but I did come in contact with some of them from time to time. It is not a study in Civil War reenacting and all the detail that goes with it. When I started out, I had a good armchair knowledge of the Civil War; but did not have any experience as a reenactor. The story has little to do with the Lakota Sioux since I was not part of any of that filming.

So what is this book about? It is about having the privilege of being a small part of a major motion picture. It is about starting in a movie and in Civil War reenacting with a clean slate. Not knowing anything adds a fresh new perspective to all encounters and experiences. It is about regular people who get thrown together in a new unfamiliar situation. It is about quickly forging lasting friendships. It is about having fun and enjoying life to the hilt. So, sit back, grab your favorite beverage, and come with me as we enter the world of background artists, where people in the background are on center stage and the major actors are in the background.

CHAPTER 1 RUINS

◆

July 20, 1994, Wednesday Evening

"Watch your step and where you put your hands. There could be rat-tlesnakes or other critters," I warned as the small group of people warily approached the ruin.

Members of the Kevin Costner Fan Club had come to South Dakota to tour *Dances With Wolves* set locations. Cindy Northup, the club's Vice President, had called and asked if I would show the club members the Civil War battlefield set. I answered I would be happy to show them the site.

Kevin Costner had filmed the *Dances With Wolves* Civil War battle scenes on a cattle ranch about twenty miles southeast of Pierre, South Dakota's capitol city. I contacted the ranch manager and received per-mission for the club's visit. Bruce Huxford who had been a reenactor in the movie also agreed to accompany the group.

Bruce and I met Philomena Ignelzi, Club President, Cindy Northup, her husband Spence, and four other members of the Kevin Costner Fan Club at their motel to take them to the Civil War site.

We drove out of Pierre following the Missouri River for twenty miles as it flowed southeast toward the Civil War site. Bruce and I discussed with the club members our work on *Dances With Wolves*, our encounters with Kevin, and our positive impressions of him. The summer evening was hot; but not as bad as it can get during July in South Dakota.

Reaching the turn-off to the movie set, we took a left off of Highway 34 and drove toward the ranch, site of *Dances With Wolves* opening Civil War scenes. It was here where the Union surgeons were going to amputate Dunbar's foot and where he escaped to make his suicide ride against the Confederate line of battle. We passed through a recently constructed cattle feeding area where back in August 1989 most of the reenactors had pitched their tents and the film company had set up the mess tent. We followed a dirt road that brought us to the open meadow where Kevin Costner staged the Civil War battle scene. The split rail fences were long gone. The Civil War farm house had collapsed in on itself and was in ruins. The ranch manager had told me he had stored hay in it and had used the upper floor as a deer stand. We drove up to the farm house ruin and climbed out of the vehicles to take a closer look at it.

Bruce and I took turns explaining the set up of the Civil War scene. We showed the locations of the Union and Confederate lines. The two shade trees that had been in front of the Confederate line still stood. The reenactors had lain under those trees to get out of the blistering sun. We showed where Kevin made his famous suicide ride against the Confederate line.

The only battle fought this day was with swarming mosquitoes. They must not have had any recent fresh blood.

The club members took plenty of pictures and plucked a few souvenir shingles from what was left of the roof. We looked for a way to cross over to the field hospital site, but could not because of the deep ravine and thick brush.

Bruce and I continued to tell stories about making *Dances With Wolves*. The club members were interested in anything dealing with Kevin Costner.

"Kevin is in Hawaii working on a futuristic movie called *Waterworld*," Philomena told us. "He wears webbed feet and hands; and his character is supposed to have gills."

It sounds strange, I thought.

Gazing out across the empty field, my mind began to wander.

How fortunate we had been to be a part of Dances With Wolves. What fun it was. What good friends we had made.

CHAPTER 2 BEGINNINGS

◆

June 25, 1989, Sunday Evening

"Rrring!"

I lunged for the telephone to cut off the loud blasts before they woke my exhausted wife and kids.

"Rrring!"

We had returned home to Pierre, South Dakota, from an all-weekend, all-school reunion in Liz's hometown of Selby, South Dakota.

"Rrring!"

"Hello?"

"Markley! How are ya? It's your old pal Pool."

"Terry, how are you? What's up?"

Terry Pool had been the assistant pastor at Faith Lutheran Church in Pierre. Terry and his family had moved several years ago to Omaha, Nebraska, where he was campus pastor with the University of Nebraska. Terry and I were close friends and enjoyed hunting, and discussing theology and American history. Terry had joined a Nebraska Civil War reenactment group, the Irish Battalion. (The group has since changed its name to the 1st Nebraska.) He had the clothing, musket, and equipment for the Civil War era. The Irish Battalion did a lot of Civil War reenacting events and had been in the movie *Glory*.

"Me and Cindy and the kids are coming to Pierre in August."

"That's great!"

"The Irish Battalion is playing Confederate infantry in a Kevin Costner movie, and I'm coming up to take part in it."

Earlier this spring, Kevin Costner made the announcement he would be directing and starring in a movie about the Old West and would be using locations in South Dakota. Current speculation was that he might choose some filming locations near Pierre.

"A couple of the guys can't make it. Are you interested in taking someone's place and being in the movie?"

Liz was now awake. I told her what Terry had just said. She thought it was a great idea.

"Just as long as I get to meet Kevin," she joked.

"Terry. Yes I'll do it!"

"We'll put together the things you'll need—musket, uniform, accouterments such as canteen, cartridge box, cap pouch. Filming begins the last week of August. I'll let you know for sure later on. They're going to pay us sixty-five dollars a day and two meals. The filming will be somewhere below Farm Island."

"This is great Terry, thanks!"

"There might be some speaking parts too."

Terry was calling other friends Dale Englemann, Tim Larson, and Bruce Huxford to see if they also wanted to be in the movie. Liz and I were excited. It was hard to sleep that night.

June 26, 1989, Monday-July 12, 1989, Wednesday

As days and then weeks passed, interest and excitement about the movie increased in Pierre, especially for those of us who would be in it. Bruce Huxford was not officially in the movie, but had been placed on the reserve list.

Three of my great-great-grandfathers had fought for the Union during the Civil War, so I had a slight trace of guilt thinking about playing a Confederate; but the war *is* over.

I took a major step toward entering the world of reenacting. No one in the Irish Battalion had a pair of Civil War era shoes that fit my small size seven feet. So I ordered a pair of brogans, the type of shoe worn by Civil War soldiers, from the C. & D. Jarnagin Company out of Corinth, Mississippi. I also decided to buy a reproduction Enfield musket from the same company. If nothing else, we might as well have a family heirloom I rationalized. Most items used by reenactors are reproductions of original clothing and equipment.

July 13, 1989, Thursday Evening

"I saw Kevin Costner out at the mall!" Liz said when I came home from work. The movie company was filming stunts on the grass behind J.C. Penney's.

I changed clothes and we drove to the mall. A slight drizzle fell. The film crew was filming from different angles how someone would appear when shot with arrows. A small crowd of onlookers watched.

We got out of our van and watched from behind the bed of a pickup truck filled with special guns, crossbows, knives, spears, and other equipment. The kids were fascinated by several bottles of fake blood. One of the crew members was unloading equipment from the back of the pickup.

"Do they mind if we stand here and watch?" Liz asked.

"Oh no," he answered. "This is enjoyable having people watch. We'll be all alone when we're working out on the prairie. We're going to get sick and tired of each other."

Kevin Costner was everywhere giving directions to the film crew.

One man had a cushion attached to his leg. A wire ran from the cushion back to a crossbow. The film crew strung an arrow lengthwise along the wire. They test fired the crossbow; the arrow traveled along the wire and hit the cushion. It worked well. They shot the arrow again, this time filming the action. The man pretended to stagger back after being hit. They attached another contraption to a man's chest. It had an arrow shaft that lay flush with his chest. When the man released a lever, the arrow shaft flipped out perpendicular from his body so it looked as if the arrow struck him in the chest.

July 14, 1989, Friday-August 5, 1989, Saturday

Terry continued to help me acquire Civil War clothing and equipment. My brogans arrived from Jarnagin's. They fit well, but were stiff as a board. It would probably take more time than I had to break in these shoes. Jack Hangar, the leader of the Irish Battalion, was making me a pair of light blue kersey wool pants. Both northern and southern armies wore these type of pants. He was also making two hats for me. They were called bummers—one blue for the Union and one gray for the Confederacy. Another member of the Irish Battalion was making a shirt for me.

I had ordered from Jarnagin's an Enfield musket, a bayonet, tin cup with a lid called a mucket, blanket, suspenders, and poncho. All the equipment arrived on time. It was great stuff.

We were letting our beards and hair grow long. I was getting the Civil War reenacting bug!

Terry told me the movie is based on a book called *Dances With Wolves* by Michael Blake. The book's title was also the Indian name of Kevin Costner's character.

We bought the book. Liz read it nonstop, then I read it. It was a good story. I was also reading *Field, Dungeon, and Escape* by Albert Richardson and *Hard Tack and Coffee* by John Billings, both authors were Civil War veterans. I wanted to get a better feel for the Civil War era and the everyday life of a soldier.

Kevin Costner was renting a house in Pierre. People saw him driving around town and shopping in the grocery store. Most everyone was polite and did not bother him. Rumor had it he liked Pierre so much he was going to buy a house here. The film crew played softball Sunday evenings at the softball complex. Sometimes Kevin would join them.

Terry found out the production company would be filming the Civil War scenes near the De Grey Access area about twenty miles southeast of Pierre on the Missouri River. He told me the Confederates would be shooting at Kevin Costner's character from behind a wall, but will be unable to hit him.

The production company telephoned and sent a follow-up letter confirming I was in the movie. The filming dates changed, and changed again. Terry called to tell us August 12th to August 19th were the final dates.

August 6, 1989, Sunday

Still no word if there was to be a place for Bruce Huxford in the movie. After church, Bruce and I drove out of town to the Pierre Gun Club to shoot my new Enfield and his Zouave. Both are 58 caliber, black-powder muzzle-loading muskets.

To fire: pour fifty grains of black powder down the muzzle, grease the minie ball, then ram it home with the ramrod. Bring the hammer back to half cock off the nipple. Place a cap on the nipple. Cock the hammer all the way back. Aim and fire.

"Kerplum!"

The musket had a kick, but less than a shotgun.

During the Civil War a good soldier could get three shots off in a minute. I would be lucky to get one shot off in three minutes. We shot seventy rounds then ran out of caps. It was great fun.

August 10, 1989, Thursday

Terry called Bruce and told him an Irish Battalion member had to drop out of the filming. There was now an opening for Bruce and he took it.

August 11, 1989, Friday

I worked at getting my gear together. Mom sent me an old pie plate, knife, and three-prong fork with bone handles to use in the movie. Bruce and I went over what we should take to the movie set. Tomorrow would be the beginning of a big event in our lives.

CHAPTER 3 CIVIL WAR

◆

August 12, 1989, Saturday

A broiling sun beat down without mercy, baking the prairie and everything on it. Stirred dust hung as thin veils in the still air. Men stood in line waiting patiently to fill out forms to work on *Dances With Wolves*.

Bruce Huxford, Dale Engelmann, and I had spent the day getting ready to go to the *Dances With Wolves* Civil War movie set. At 4:30 p.m., we left Pierre and drove twenty miles southeast to the Civil War set near the De Grey public access area on the Missouri River.

After locating the first arrivals of the Irish Battalion from Omaha, and signing the movie company's forms, we learned of an immediate problem. Where would the Irish Battalion be allowed to set up camp? The Irish Battalion had brought their Civil War era tents to be used as part of the field hospital set. We were to set up the tents on the movie set; we also needed to sleep in them. The film people originally said we could camp at the field hospital set; but now they told us, we could not. The Irish Battalion representative told the film representative we needed to sleep in the tents since we had no other place to stay. The film representative finally gained permission for us to sleep in our tents on the field hospital set.

We got into our vehicles to drive out to the set. The set director stopped us. We could not drive there since they had eliminated all modern vehicle tracks and foot prints.

The film representative told us they were bringing a team of horses and a wagon down from the Houck Buffalo Ranch. The Houck Ranch northwest of Pierre was the location of the Ft. Sedgewick and the buffalo hunt sets. The wagon would haul the tents and our gear to the hospital set. It would take several hours for the team and wagon to get here; it would be dark; and we had no guarantee they would take our gear up to the set. We decided to sleep out under the stars and head out to the set tomorrow. The film representative gave us permission to sleep under the large mess tent tonight.

I opened my cooler and passed out beer and pop to the Irish Battalion members. Reenactors were arriving from all over the country. Members of the 1st Virginia from San Jose`, California, came over to talk.

Virginia Confederates in California? I mused.

They knew the Irish Battalion from the 125th anniversary reenactment of the battle of Gettysburg.

Katzell
1989

Quick
Sketch

House on the confederate side
of the battle field

of the set "Dances with wolves"

Rainy Sunday morning   August 19, 1989
South Dakota

The Irish Battalion people had brought a pair of pants Jack Hanger had made for me. Jack had not hemmed the pants since he did not know my pant length. Nothing was going on, so Dale and I drove back to Pierre. We stopped at my house to drop off the pants which Liz was willing to hem.

We grabbed a bite to eat, picked up more beer, and drove back to the film set. The security guards, off-duty Pierre police officers, let us through the gate.

Jack Hanger, the leader of the Irish Battalion, had arrived. He was a large man with a dark beard and deep voice. I introduced myself to him. He told me he was portraying a rebel colonel and was in charge of all Confederate troops. Jack said on the job he was second to Andy Cannon in the hiring and firing of people and deciding if what they wore was historically accurate. Andy Cannon was the reenactor coordinator from Victor, Montana.

It was good to sleep outside. I lay between two loud snorers, who kept it up most of the night. Two boisterous men walked through our sleeping, snoring group before they realized we were there.

August 13, 1989, Sunday

We got up at daylight to allow the caterers to set up for breakfast; but the caterers and food never arrived. The film company had not told them to feed us on Sunday. Jack was given meal money for the Irish Battalion. So we drove to the Country Kitchen Restaurant in Pierre for breakfast.

When our waitress learned we were working on *Dances With Wolves*, she made a big fuss over us. By the time we left the restaurant, everyone knew we were going to be in the movie.

Back at the movie set, the film representative allowed us to drive a few vehicles up to the field hospital site. We consolidated the tents and our gear into three vehicles and drove out toward the site.

The dirt road led to the Union side of the Civil War battle set. A large deflated balloon was draped in the trees to our right. It was to appear shot down by the Confederates. The road continued straight along an open grassy field; but we took a left on an intersecting dirt road. To the left of the road was a large shady tree. Civil War era equipment sat on top of a wooden table beneath the tree. Alongside the table was a pile of apples on the ground. To the right a split rail fence separated the road from the large field. Cooking fires, pots, pans, and various utensils and equipment had been placed between the road and the fence.

Beyond the rail fence, the wide field ran for about two hundred yards to a second split rail fence where the Confederate troops will be. The field was level with a few depressions in it. Several tree stumps poked their stubs up above the grass. Three black and white Holstein cows lay dead in the field. They were fake.

A two-story frame farmhouse stood behind the rail fence on the far side of the field. It was built for the movie and had been copied from a Civil War era photo. It looked as if it had been hit by cannon fire. Old tattered curtains hung in windows with broken panes.

A pile of corn cobs was on the left side of the house; an apple pile was to the right of the house. To the right were outbuildings and a buggy. An outhouse and small vegetable garden were to the left of the house.

Where trees were not wanted, the set crew cut them down. Where trees were wanted, the set crew dug holes and planted full-grown trees. The scene was to take place in the autumn, so the set crew had spray-painted the trees' leaves to give them fall colors.

We drove to the end of the fence line and entered a tree covered ravine. The road wound up a steep incline on the other side of the ravine and came out at a large level field lined with trees. This was the field hospital site and where we set up camp.

The field hospital was a series of tents to the right of the road. Antiques from the 1860's were positioned around the camp. It looked like a scene from out of the Civil War. All that was needed were the people to make it complete.

Here the first scene of the movie was to take place. Kevin Costner's character is wounded in the foot. The doctors are getting ready to amputate Dunbar's foot and he escapes.

The film representative told us to set up our camp on the left side of the road across from the field hospital tents. We were not to touch anything in the field hospital. It was off limits to the Irish Battalion.

We had to have the vehicles off the set as fast as we could; so we quickly unloaded the tents and our gear. From now on, no motorized vehicles would be allowed to come up the road. We began to set up the tents aligned in rows and facing the hospital tents so they would be visible to the movie cameras.

The tents were difficult to set up. Fortunately some of the people knew what they were doing and instructed the rest of us.

Tim Larson arrived by way of an old army hospital wagon pulled by a pair of mules. The wagon brought the rest of the tents. The driver was R.L. Curtin from Montana.

We were hot and sweaty. Tim took a break from working on the tents to fill his canteen with water from a wooden water cask. A man with the movie crew walked up to him.

"How's it going?" he asked.

"Good!" Tim replied. They talked for some time. Tim later realized he had been talking with Kevin Costner.

The mules and wagon returned with Kevin's wife Cindy and two of their three children. She thanked us for helping get the set ready.

Three men were to sleep in each tent. Bruce, Tim, and Dale were together in one tent. I shared a tent with two Nebraskans, Bill Deardorff and Jason, a tall skinny kid. Bill was a few years younger than me. Bill and I discovered we both had been to the Antarctic. He had been to The Ice with the Coast Guard in 1980 while I was there as a civilian working on a scientific research project in 1972 and 1973. I found out later that night, Bill snores loudly and Jason talks and shouts in his sleep.

Jack Hangar told us to get dressed in our Civil War uniforms and accouterments. They were going to inspect us to make sure we looked authentic. Jack Provines, Bill, and Jason showed Bruce, Tim, Dale, and me how to dress and put on the accouterments.

I took off my modern day clothes and pulled on long johns that I had cut off at the knees. While not the coolest underwear, it would help prevent chaffing. I put on cotton socks and then gray wool socks. I pulled a long-sleeved print cotton shirt over my head. The shirt was of one piece and had three buttons in the front at the top. I then put on the baggy kersey wool pants. When wearing the pants, they are to be up to the belly button. No zipper at the fly, only metal buttons. Suspenders held up the pants; there were no belt loops for a belt. My new brogan shoes were still stiff and felt as if it would take a week to break them in. Next I put on a gray wool shell jacket and buttoned it all the way up to my neck. I jammed the gray bummer down tight on top of my head.

My leather cartridge box and strap were slung over my left shoulder with the box on my right hip. I fastened the leather waist-belt around my middle. The cap box was attached to the right side of the belt and the bayonet in its scabbard hung from the belt on my left side. We were not to use any of our musket caps or cartridges; the production company would supply these to us. The haversack hung over my right shoulder and rested on my left hip. The haversack contained all the soldier's essentials. In my case this included: camera, extra film, snacks, journal and plenty of pens. The bulls-eye canteen was also hung over the right shoulder and rested on top of the haversack. We were to always keep water in our canteens. A rolled-up blanket was draped over the left shoulder with the two ends tied together and reached to the right hip. I attached my tin cup to the haversack's keeper strap. The last item I picked up was my Enfield musket. I was ready to plunge into the Civil War.

At 4:00 p.m., we formed up on the road in a single line by size—the taller to the right, the shorter to the left. I stood close to the left end of the line. We counted off by two's and formed up into two lines.

"Right shoulder arms!" shouted Jack. "Right face! March step! March!"

We marched down the road to the mess tent. Colonel Jack Hangar rode ahead on his horse. The Confederate stars and bars and battle flag flew next. Then the troops came marching along. There was a constant clanging of tin cups hitting bayonets, the tramp of feet, and talk among the men. The wool uniforms were hot and sweaty. The multitude of feet stirred up a huge cloud of dust over us.

We arrived at the mess tent late. The other reenactors were camped right there and did not have to walk a half mile to get there. Each of us was handed a script of the upcoming Civil War scenes.

Kevin Costner was giving a pep talk to the two-hundred-and-fifty reenactors. This was the first movie he had ever directed and needed our help to make it look good. There were a lot of people who were saying it would not work; but he hoped we could pull it off. As Kevin began to leave, the people playing Yankees mobbed him for his autograph.

We were inspected to ensure we had the proper uniforms and equipment. Most people passed. After this, the Confederate troops were drilled in forming ranks, marching, and various commands. The Irish Battalion drilled with the other Confederates who were camping down below. The largest Confederate contingent was the 1st Virginia from California. Everyone was to carry, load, and fire his musket right-handed. This was awkward for me since I am left-handed and have always shot left-handed.

After drill, we drove to Pierre, still wearing our uniforms and ate at the Golden Corral Restaurant. We stopped at the Red Owl grocery and department store to buy a few things. People stared wherever we went. We returned to the set and walked back to camp.

It was getting late and Terry Pool had not arrived. The senior pastor of his church had died and Terry had to conduct Sunday services. He had said he would not arrive at the movie set until Sunday night. I figured he was probably not going to make it tonight and was starting to get ready for bed when I heard his voice in the dark and then Tim Larson's wife, Jan and Liz's voices. Jan and Liz were helping Terry carry his gear up to the camp in the dark. They were given the wrong directions and had walked to the battlefield set farmhouse. Seeing our lights, they followed a ravine until it ran into the road to our camp. Terry dropped his gear and gave me a big bear-hug.

Jack Hangar did not think it proper for women to be in camp. Tim and I were soon escorting our wives back down to the gate. At least they had a chance to see the set, even though it was in the dark. My mother-in-law, Helen Swift, was in the van watching our young children, Becky and Chris, and trying to keep them quiet. They were going to Sioux Falls tomorrow for a two-day shopping expedition. Tim and I kissed our wives goodbye and hiked back to camp.

Terry was getting situated in the tent he was sharing with Chuck Dail, a Captain in the Irish Battalion. Tim went to bed while Terry offered me a pipe of tobacco and some Irish whiskey to get in the mood for the Civil War. We had a good talk and then went to bed.

The night was warm and clear. It was hard to get to sleep. I could hear Larry Trout, another member of the Irish Battalion, and Jack talking during the lull in Bill's loud snoring to my right and Jason's monologue to my left.

August 14, 1989, Monday

5:30 a.m., "Reveille!" Terry shouted. We had a half hour of half-light to dress, find our equipment, and form ranks out in front of the tents on the Company Street.

What have I gotten myself into? I thought which is probably the question most new recruits ask themselves at reveille. Only partly awake, I tried to dress and put on all the unfamiliar equipment.

6:00 a.m., we formed up on the Company Street. With flags flying, we marched down the dirt road to breakfast. We formed ranks with the other Confederate troops who were waiting for us.

"Fix bayonets!" Colonel Hangar ordered and then "Stack arms!" This was a tricky process I was never able to master. Two muskets are leaned against each other at the bottom of the bayonet and then a third is inserted underneath to form a tripod. They are twisted in one direction to lock. The fourth musket is leaned against the tripod and it should not fall over. Should not! "The saying goes 'Any man who drops his musket must sleep with it,'" Terry announced to the assembled troops. The flags were furled and laid across the tops of the musket tripods.

We marched double file to the caterer's truck where they handed out breakfast in Styrofoam containers—scrambled eggs and ham. We walked to the mess tent to find empty spots at the tables to sit down and eat. I got one cup of coffee before it was gone. Some people were complaining about the food.

Beggars can't be choosy, I thought. *This food's great. We're getting $55 a day, two meals, and $10 for supper. Not bad!*

Dale Oakley was the Confederate drummer. He was from Ohio and played in the movie *North and South*. His drum was over one hundred years old.

"It's hard to get good tone on the drum in the morning because of the dampness. I need to hold it over a fire to dry it out." Dale started playing the drum, even though he and Jack had had an argument earlier over drums.

"Drums give me a headache!" Jack declared.

"A good drummer will not give you a headache," Dale answered.

Jack gave the orders to form up, take arms, and march to makeup. The Yankees shouted catcalls and snide remarks as we marched past them.

The 1st Virginia had a fife player. He and Dale began to play southern tunes. We sang along with "Dixie", but were rather weak and only a few people knew the words to "Bonnie Blue Flag". The Yankees sang

"Dixie" after us only much louder and stronger. We would have to work on our singing.

The makeup people worked through the lines of men. They put brown makeup on our faces and hands to make sure we looked sun-tanned. They smudged black powder on our faces and hands to look like powder burns. They rubbed glycerin in our hair to make it look greasy. They hit our clothes with dust bags to make them look dirty.

When makeup was through with us, we marched down the dusty road past the Union lines, and across the meadow to the far fence in front of the farmhouse. We were positioned along the fence and told to hold those positions. The 1st Virginia was to the far left in front of the farmhouse. The flags were placed almost dead center between the 1st Virginia and us. I was by a large stump to the right of the flags. Most of the Irish Battalion was to my right. I was separated from Bruce, Tim, Dale, and Terry; they were far to my right. I was to the left of the center position from the camera's viewpoint.

Don Patrick from Maryland was on my left and on my right was Tom Flanigan from Montana. We would get to know each other very well as the days went on, for as you will see, we did not change positions much.

Even though the morning sky was overcast and there was a cool breeze, my wool uniform was hot.

Neal Vickery and Chuck portrayed officers and sat by an imaginary campfire behind me. When the film crew wanted a fire, they had us start a small smoker to provide the campfire smoke.

The scene was supposed to be early morning with fog. To get the fog effect, the film crew would start up a large smoke machine that resembled an everglades airboat.

Don was very funny and told many jokes. One of his favorite sayings was, using a southern accent, "I'm fighting for my rights!" Only with the accent it sounded like "I'm fightin' for my rats!" This sent everyone into a tirade of rat sayings and stories.

I told my favorite rat tale that took place when my brother Doug and I were kids on the farm in Pennsylvania. It was a cold, snowy winter evening. Doug and I went to the corncrib to shell corn to feed the animals. We used an old hand-cranked corn sheller. We always first banged the shoot where the shelled corn would come out to make sure there were no little critters in there; but that evening we forgot. I would get the machine cranked up by spinning the handle that would turn the internal gears and disks that stripped the kernels from the cobs. It was a two-holer so Doug was ready to put two ears of corn in after I got the machine revved up. As I turned the crank, the gears and disks hit something and caught. There was a high pitched squeal. A rat flew out the shoot and landed on the upper part of my left leg. I could feel his little claws poke through my jeans and into my leg. The rat and I stared at each other. The hair stood on the back of my neck. I don't know who was more terrified the rat or me. It was only a second or two before he sprang from my leg and ran off; but it seemed as if time stood still as he hung there on my leg.

Kevin Costner rode up to us on his horse.

"Did all of you read the script that was handed out last night?"

There was a mass murmur of "Yes."

"I know you don't like to run; but this is a scene I really need to make the movie work. When I was in the movie *No Way Out*, I had to play the part of a Russian spy which I didn't like."

He explained what would happen in the scene. Lieutenant Dunbar rides toward the Confederate line to die in front of the rebel guns. He rides straight at the line. Eight men in the center fire and miss him. He rides across in front of the Confederate right where I am. We shoot at him, one right after the other. Don is the first to shoot, then me, then Tom and so on down the line. We do not hit Dunbar. He stops; we coax him back. He rides back; but most of us are not prepared to fire. Just one or two get shots off. He rides by the Confederate left who stand as a firing squad. They all shoot at once and miss. The Yankees will charge and before we can reload; they are on us and push us back through the cornfield into the trees.

"Well boys, carry on here," Kevin finished. "I have to go back to the other side of the field and make the girls cry."

Dave Silva, the assistant director in charge of the Confederates, was dressed as a Confederate officer. He was visible during the filming of the Confederate line and was in constant communication with Kevin and the rest of the film crew by way of a small two-way earphone and microphone. Dave was friendly and worked well with us.

For this first scene Dave told us to slowly mill around as if we were tired and bored after fighting for a long time. The film crew turned on the smoke machine to make it look like early morning fog. Dave positioned each of us and told us we should always do the same actions each time the filming began. I started out the scene sitting by the fence, standing up, and walking over to the fake campfire where Neal and Chuck are sitting. I talk with them and pour myself a pretend cup of coffee.

The crew filmed this scene several times. The Union troops were doing the same types of actions as the Confederates. Up on a far hill, the Union general and his staff stood together on horseback. The crew filmed them with us as background. In front of the General and his staff were rows of corn; but this corn was different. The set crew had stapled fresh corn stalks to two-by-fours in rows, so they could move the cornstalks when they needed to change the scene.

One of the classic people on the Confederate line was a crusty old character, Dave "Bullet" Wooters from Montana. Bullet was originally from Maryland's Eastern Shore and was a true-blue rebel. He wore little spectacles perched on his nose and had a long red beard and long scraggly hair. A rounded short-brimmed hat was jauntily tipped over one eye. He knew an awful lot about the Civil War—what was correct to wear, do, and say. He did a lot of cutting up. "I can't believe all you Yankees pretending to be Confederates!" Bullet told us. He was chosen

Quick
Sketch

HATZELL
1989

UNION SOLDIER
RENDEZVOUS MONDAY MORNING
AUGUST 14, 1989
ON THE MOVIE SET "DANCES WITH WOLVES"

to try out for the part of a sharpshooter; but when the film crew looked him over, "They told me I wasn't ugly enough!" We laughed since he had a lot of character in his face and was very ornery. We wondered who could have beaten him.

Bill Blake was another character also from the eastern shore of Maryland. Bill and Bullet had known each other in Maryland. When those two got together it was fun to listen to their banter back and forth.

The crew filmed the scene of Lieutenant Dunbar riding to the Confederate lines and being shot at as he passed in front of us. They would film his return ride along the line later. Kevin's double did this ride. He had played the part of one of the kids in the John Wayne movie *The Cowboys*. After several shots of this ride, it was early afternoon and time for lunch.

We formed up and marched back to the mess tent. The Yankees got to the food first and ate all the pies before we could get any. This made many of the Confederates angry. Our battle cry after this was not "The South shall rise again!" but "Remember the pies!".

It was hot and dusty. The food and drinks were good; but again, some people complained. The film crew and major actors ate separate from us.

The outhouses were foul and very full. The stench was bad. Thousands of buzzing flies filled the air. I can see how disease spread rapidly during the Civil War.

We marched back out to the set and spent the rest of the day filming over and over again Dunbar's ride along the Confederate line. The film crew used various camera angles and lenses.

One way the crew filmed us was by using a camera mounted on a vehicle that drove in front of and along the fence line. They filmed us from the vehicle as we shot at an imaginary Dunbar. They told us to aim and shoot at the vehicle. "US" in large letters was painted on the side of the vehicle.

We held a lengthy philosophical discussion. If they are "US", are we "THEM"?

It was so hot in our wool uniforms. The craft services people brought ice and water out to us; but it was never enough. The water and ice were set up behind the farmhouse out of sight of the cameras.

Many people were getting chigger bites from lying in the green grass under the trees in front of the fence. I was fortunate and did not get any bites; but my right shoe was rubbing my ankle the wrong way and soon the skin was off.

Filming was over by 7:00 p.m. We marched back to the field in front of the mess tent where we were drilled in marching and various formations. We then marched back to camp and were dismissed.

Tim drove Terry, Dale, Bruce, and me in his pickup back to Pierre. Dale and I rode in the back of the truck.

You can't get a view of the whole sky, river, and countryside like this cooped up in the cab, I thought.

Tim dropped Dale and Bruce off at their houses. Liz had left for Sioux Falls, so Terry and I took showers at Lila Houck's house, since that was where Terry's wife Cindy and children were staying.

We went to the D&E Café for supper. The D&E was my all-time favorite greasy spoon. It was only a hole-in-the-wall establishment; but the food was always good and cheap. I would tell people who had never been there "It's a piece of Americana you have to experience." The place was busy and noisy as usual. I had my usual—a club steak, potatoes, salad, toast, coffee, all for under three dollars.

Everyone was in bed by the time we got back to the set. I went to sleep right away.

August 15, 1989, Tuesday

The morning routine was similar to Monday's.
5:30 a.m., reveille.

6:00 a.m., march to breakfast.

The Yankees continued to annoy us. Yesterday they ate all the pies; today they drank all the coffee before we could get our fill. One Yankee butted in line a few people ahead of me and filled a large tin cup to the brim with the hot steaming brew. The coffee urns were nearly empty when I reached them. I was fortunate with a half cup.

More! whined my caffeine-deprived brain.

After eating, we marched to Makeup. After Makeup applied Hollywood suntan to our faces, grease to our hair, and dirt to our clothes, we marched out to the set to the beat of the drum and the playing of the fife. We sang "Dixie" and "Bonny Blue Flag" better than yesterday. People stopped what they were doing and watched as we marched by singing and the flags streaming ahead of us.

Back on the Confederate line, we took the same positions we held yesterday. The film crew concentrated on filming the Confederate left in front of the farmhouse. People on my end of the line, talked and catnapped. I made more new friends.

Lunch was miserable. The wind came up strong, blowing dirt into our food and drink. The craft services crew provided plenty of liquids and ice on the set all day.

The film crew filmed us coaxing Dunbar to ride back along the Confederate line. Kevin worked on this filming and then returned to the Union side to work on the scene where Dunbar jumps his horse over the fence and out onto the field. When we wave for Dunbar to ride back along the Confederate line, I am waving my ramrod in the air.

The day was very hot. Wool uniforms did not help. When not working, reenactors looked for any shade they could find. One of the best spots was two small shade trees in the pasture in front of our fence. Up to twenty people would be stretched out in the shade, sleeping or talking. Grown men spent their idle time shredding leaves, peeling the bark off twigs, and whittling sticks. Don made me a little pistol out of a twig. Terry gave me a small telescope he made out of a corncob.

RATZELL
1989

Quick
Sketch
"TUCKER"
RENDERED ON LOCATION OF
THE FILM "DANCES WITH WOLVES"
WEDNESDAY AUGUST 16, 1989

"What do you do for a living?" Don lazily asked himself. "Well, I peel the bark off of twigs and shred leaves."

The set crew were scattering boxes and boxes of dead leaves for close up scenes.

"Where do they get the leaves?" I asked a set crew member as he was scattering them on the ground.

"They were shipped in from North Carolina," he answered. The set crew spray painted vegetation brown or green depending on what was needed for a scene.

"What do you do for a living?" Don again asked himself . "Why I spray paint grass and weeds and scatter dried dead leaves on the ground."

Frank Costanza, a Montana bootmaker, played the part of Sergeant Tucker. During the filming, Frank says a few words and gallops his horse behind the Confederate lines. Sometimes Frank had trouble remembering where and when to start his horse or where to stop. The film crew fixed this by placing markers on the ground.

The crew had us prepare for a specialty shot. Thirteen of us stood in line and were to fire down the line, one right after the other. A camera was set on a track and moved past each of us as we took the shot. The only thing the camera would see would be the musket barrel and the muzzle flash as we fired. They had to be very precise as to where we were placed and at what elevation our muskets were at. I made little depressions in the ground where my feet were to be. This took one and a half hours to set up in the hot sun. We had to hold our muskets out in the firing position for long periods of time. It was very tiring, hot work. Finally, the film crew was set and ready to go. They got a call that all cameras had to be back on the Union line for Kevin's jump shot. They tried to explain the scene was all set. The shot would be over in fifteen minutes; but our film crew did not prevail. So they tore down the cameras and went over to the Dunbar jump scene. We never did do that shot.

It was now evening and all filming was on the Union side. We were very tired at the end of the day as we marched back to camp.

Instead of driving to town, we decided to go for a swim in the Missouri River at the De Grey access area and eat food we had brought along. Eight of us crammed into the cab and piled into the back of Tim's pickup truck for the short ride over to the access area.

We picked our way down to the water's edge over sharp rocks and driftwood, past the remains of a carp. As we swam in the cool, murky water, Terry had a revelation.

"Let's organize a lodge. We can call it—the Royal Order of Raccoons!" We thought it was a great idea and became Founding Fathers on the spot. Terry's fertile mind began working overtime in a free flow of ideas about the Lodge. The rest of us chimed in from time to time with improvements and embellishments.

"We have to have a secret signal so Brother Raccoons can recognize each other," Terry mused. A few minutes later he said "How about—this!" and placed his hand palm down on the top of his head and waved his fingers out front. "Then all Brother Raccoons must make the signal back."

We liked it, approved it, and practiced it.

"When should we make the sign?" a Founding Father asked.

"When a Brother breaks wind!"

It was unanimous.

"And when someone belches!"

A chorus of "yes!"

"Or when you pop the top of a beer can!"

More affirmation.

"Or pop."

Again mass agreement.

We made up all kinds of rules and elected Terry Grand Puba since the Lodge was his brainchild.

The Grand Puba spoke. "I think new member initiation should be that the neophyte must dive into the water at De Grey, feel through the muck with his whiskers for shellfish, and then surface with a shellfish between his teeth." We shot down that idea. We agreed upon a more simple method—a majority secret vote of Brothers. The candidate must close his eyes while the Lodge Brothers take a silent vote. No one would ever be excluded; but they would be told "It was a close vote; but you're in."

Outhouses would be lodge buildings and toilettes would be thrones. A roll of toilet paper would be the sacred scroll. The full moon was the "Great Shellfish in the Sky". Best of all no membership dues.

During the week, we inducted all the Confederates into the Lodge and a good many Yankees and film crew. Several reenactors tried to get Kevin Costner to join; but he said "You need to be more selective." He did once make the hand sign not knowing what he was doing. One of the Yankee Brothers was signaling to a Film Crew Brother who was standing behind Kevin. Kevin thought the Yankee Brother was waving to him and he made the sign back.

We returned to the set where we were told we could start a fire at the field hospital set, as long as we dug a fire pit. Each of us grabbed an armful of wood and hiked up the dusty road to our camp.

Our jolly band sat around a blazing campfire eating a makeshift supper of cheese, crackers, apples, and sardines and washing it down with beer. Terry passed around his bottle of Irish whiskey. Chuck handed out cigars. We had plenty of practice using our new Royal Order of Raccoon hand signal as the Great Shellfish in the Sky slowly rose overhead.

August 16, 1989, Wednesday

5:30 a.m. arrived too early. I was more asleep than awake. Using the morning's dim light, Bill, Jason, and I rummaged in the cramped tent for our Civil War era clothes and accouterments. It was getting easier to find my clothing and gear, since I was learning to make sure everything was ready and in its proper place the night before.

Quick
Sketches
of a very busy actor/director
Kevin Costner

Rendered on the film set of
"Dances with wolves"
Wednesday August 16, 1989   Susan Dawson

Again the Irish Battalion went through the same routine as Monday and Tuesday: form ranks on the Company Street in front of the tents, route step march down the dusty road to the mess tent, and eat a hearty breakfast. We marched to Makeup where they made sure we looked suntanned, dirty, and greasy; and then we marched out to the set.

An assistant director stopped us and had us line up on the Union side of the set. He asked if anyone wanted to play the part of a Union Major. Doc, a member of the Irish Battalion, was the only one to raise his hand. The film crew took him. The rest of the Confederates good naturally called after him "Traitor!" and "Galvanized Yankee!"

After reaching the Confederate line and taking our positions, Jack told me to take Doc's place. Doc had been in the center position of the Confederate line and was the sixth person to shoot at Dunbar when he first rides towards the Confederate line.

The eight people who first shot at Dunbar called themselves "The Straight Eight" since they could not shoot straight. I became the ninth member of "The Straight Eight".

In my new position, I was to squat by a fire with other Confederates. As filming begins, we notice Dunbar riding towards us. I stand up and run to my musket leaning against the fence. I pick up the musket, aim at Dunbar, fire, and of course miss.

The crew filmed this scene of Dunbar riding toward us over and over again from a variety of angles using different cameras and lens. I got to know Terry Hall, a farmer from Bruce, South Dakota, and Paul Williams, a rancher from Long Valley, South Dakota, who were both members of "The Straight Eight".

The makeup people examined our appearance when the cameras were not rolling. They made sure we looked good and dirty by slapping our clothes with dirt bags. Brigitta Bjerke, the costume supervisor, was an older woman from Sweden. Brigitta thoroughly enjoyed her job. She was constantly laughing and joking with us as she made sure we looked extra dirty by hitting us repeatedly with the dirt bags.

Again there was a lot of filming and a lot of waiting in the hot sun. Some shots were close-ups.

After lunch, one of the specialty shots was the shooting of "Ray". Just as Ray, the Confederate sharpshooter, has Lieutenant Dunbar in his sights and is squeezing the trigger, he is shot in the head. The film crew selected a San Jose`, California, firefighter with the 1st Virginia Regiment to portray Ray and paid him eight-hundred dollars to do the stunt. The film crew created the head wound by shooting red paint from a paint gun onto Ray's forehead from a few feet away. They hooked him up to a harness and a cable was attached to the back of the harness. Film crew members jerked Ray backwards after the shot in the head. Kevin personally worked on setting up this scene. It took a long time to get it just right. Ray had to be in the exact spot. The cameras had to be in exact position. Everyone had to move with split-second timing. A great amount of time and effort went into this one brief shot. I found out years later, the Union soldier who shoots Ray in the film was Kevin Costner's father.

The crew set up for the last major scene of the day. The Yankees were to leave their position and charge part way out into the field and then stop. But as the crew continued to film the same scene over and over again, the Yankees came all the way up to our fence, especially the cavalry. None of them ever died as they charged our line. They were belligerent, yelling at us to run or die like dogs. They were trying to demoralize us; but only made us angry. As they charged us again and again, we stood our ground. I wondered what I would have done in a real battle of that kind. Would I stand or run?

We were sick and tired of the Yankees' actions—eating all the pies, drinking all the coffee, the snide remarks, and now this belligerent charging our line. Their actions were not part of the film. Jack was angry.

"The next time they charge, if they go past the depression in the field, I'll have the bugler blow the bugle. That will mean load, fire a volley over their heads, come back to the ready position with fixed bayonets, and stand your ground!" he said.

The officers passed the word down the line.

The Yankees charged at a full run. Over a hundred screaming men ran at us with fixed bayonets. The cameras were filming off to the left in the middle of the field. Kevin watched the action on his horse behind the cameras We stood with fixed bayonets silently waiting for the Yankees. They reached the depression, did not stop, and continued to run toward us. The bugler sounded the signal. Each man quickly tore open a blank cartridge, poured the black powder down the barrel, and primed his musket. On command the entire Confederate line erupted in a massed volley. What a mighty roar and cloud of smoke billowed from our muskets.

The Yankee charge stopped dead in its tracks. Two-thirds of the troops dropped to the ground. Some just stood where they stopped. A few ran up to our fence. We told them they were our prisoners. Many dropped since they knew they should take a hit as good reenactors. Others dropped to the ground since they did not know if we were really firing at them or not. Some were just plain tired and it was a good excuse to lay down. One officer dropped on top of a red ant hill. The ants swarmed into his clothes and attacked. He was madly trying to strip off his clothes. None of the Yankees or film crew had known we were going to fire that volley.

"If I get fired over this, so be it," Jack said.

A shout "Three cheers for the colonel!"

The entire Confederate line waved their hats in the air and roared at the top of their lungs "Hip Hip Hooray! Hip Hip Hooray! Hip Hip Hooray!"

Another shout "Let's hear it for the Yanks!"

The line cheered again "Hip Hip Hooray!"

We felt great.

Kevin stern faced came galloping on his horse from the cameras toward the Confederate line.

Was he angry? Would we be fired?

He reined his horse to a stop in front our fence and shook his fist at us. "You guys are killers!" he shouted. "You're all a bunch of killers!"

Then he broke into a big grin and galloped back to the cameras. The Confederate line roared with cheers again.

Later, Bill, a blond long-haired cameraman, told me "You guys took the crew totally by surprise. We have the whole thing on camera."

Jack had not been popular with some of the troops because of his strict discipline; but after the unauthorized volley, everyone thought he was great. Morale was at an all time high. We would now be able to go through the retreat scenes with pride.

Filming was over for the day. We gathered our gear, and formed ranks four abreast. Jack rode ahead on his horse, followed by the flag bearers, then the drummer and fifer, and next the two companies of Confederate troops. I do not think we ever marched better or sang louder. People stood at the side of the road smiling, waving, and taking pictures.

We had a short meeting back at the mess tent and were told not to fire again without being told. We broke ranks for the night.

Tim gave Terry and me a ride into town in his pickup. We did not change out of our Confederate uniforms. We stopped at Lila Houck's house. Lila said everyone was at Bob and Nancy Shoup's house for Nancy's birthday. We decided to crash the party in our uniforms. We climbed into Lila's pickup and she drove us to the party. Everyone was surprised to see us, especially in uniform. My wife, Liz, and our kids, Becky and Chris were glad to see me. Later, Nancy told us one of her neighbors thought Tim was Kevin Costner.

Liz drove me home after cake and ice cream. It was great to take a good hot bath and eat hot home cooked food.

Tim picked me up at 11:30 p.m. As we headed back out to the set, we witnessed an eclipse of the full moon. We hiked the dirt road back up to camp and turned in for the night.

August 17, 1989, Thursday

Again the same routine as before. While we waited for breakfast, four Yankees butted in line. Chuck complained to their Captain; but he did nothing about it.

Today was a slow day for us. We did not work until 4:00 p.m.; but we had to remain on the set the entire time. The crew spent most of the day filming the scene after the battle, when the Union General sends for his physician to help Dunbar.

I met Kevin Costner's father, Bill. He liked Pierre and has had an enjoyable time here. He said "The only time Kevin has been bothered was when two men from Sioux Falls stopped by the house and wanted to talk to him on a Sunday morning when he was still sleeping."

The following is a real-time sketch of what was happening and what I was thinking during the afternoon.

> The crew is setting up to film Kevin Costner lying in the grass after he falls from his horse. The Confederate troops positioned in front of the old house retreat on our left.
>
> I am four fence lengths to the right of the Confederate flags, sitting with my back to the fence. Horses are picketed in front of me. Jack Hangar is trying to sleep to my right. Dave Baumann from Colorado is sleeping on my left. Farther to the left Don Patrick, Bill Blake and Brian Stewart discuss the Royal Order of Raccoons and the use of the hand signal. The few people not sleeping are watching the filming.
>
> Bill Blake walking by stops to talk with me.
>
> "I'm amazed you Westerners are playing Confederates and doing a right good job of it. What are you writing?"
>
> "I'm trying to keep a diary."

HATZELL 1989

Quick
Sketches

Rendered on the film set of
" DANCES WITH WOLVES "
Thursday August 17, 1989
Santa Barbara

"If you hang around with the Marylanders you'll hear some right choice words to write." He walks away chuckling.

I have heard a lot of jokes, some good and some not so good.

The Yankees are across the field. I can hear them drilling. Some of them have been butting in the food lines, eating all the dessert, and making snide remarks about how they are going to wipe us out.

A shout, "Cut!"

The sky is cloudy. A stiff breeze snaps the flags. The film crew does not like how strong the wind is blowing.

"We have Chapters in several states," Larry Trout is explaining the Royal Order of Raccoons to Clyde Kocher.

The Yankees are now marching down the road to the beat of the drums.

A grinning Bill Blake returns from the scene of Dunbar lying on the ground after he falls from his horse. "Costner's horse dropped a load of road apples and missed Kevin's head by a foot! The film crew couldn't help but laugh!" he tells me.

I am getting a little taste of what the Civil War must have been like—a lot of hurry up and wait. The wool uniforms are hot and heavy; but everyone is in good humor.

During the filming of one of the scenes, Frank Costanza's horse reared up and threw Frank to the ground, dislocating his shoulder. They had to find a double to take his place.

We had to do a retreat scene back from the fence and into the corn-field. It was an orderly retreat until we reached the corn, then we were supposed to run.

Late in the day, Doc returned to our lines. "They decided to use some-one else as the major instead of me," Doc said. He went back to his posi-tion with The Straight Eight and I went back to my original position.

When people watch the movie, won't they wonder why certain people disappear from spots and pop up in other places? I thought.

We spent more time lying and talking under the shade trees. Dave Baumann from Colorado was sketching the farmhouse. It looked good.

One Californian with the 1st Virginia was a strange character. He car-ried a fly swatter with him at all times. We nicknamed him "Fly Boy." The 1st Virginians told us Fly Boy spent most of the day in the farm-house, swatting flies. He bragged he had killed over one thousand flies in the farmhouse. During one of the breaks, Fly Boy was sleeping on the corncobs piled against the house. Kids from the 1st Virginia took his fly swatter and hid it. When he woke up and discovered it was missing, he went berserk until he got his fly swatter back.

We finished the day about 8:00 p.m. I took Bill Blake, Dale Oakley, and Brian Stewart to town for showers and supper. Brian was from Minnesota and had been hired to play the banjo in one of the scenes. Bill had not been off the movie set since he did not have a car. He was not impressed with the small portion of South Dakota he had seen, so I drove them up to Oahe dam. They were impressed. Oahe Dam is the second largest earthen dam in the world. The Aswan Dam on the Nile River is the largest. Bill changed his opinion of South Dakota, but still would not want to live here.

We dropped Dale off at the Super 8 Motel where he was staying and then drove to the YMCA for showers. It was 9:30 p.m.; the staff was closing up for the night. They refused to let us in. We pleaded with them and assured them we would be quick. They relented and let us into the building. There is nothing like a good hot shower when you are hot, dirty, and tired.

We were ravenous so we went to the D&E Café for supper. Jack, Chuck, and Larry were eating there.

I stopped by the house to see Liz and the kids. Then we drove back out to the set. The security guard gave me a ride up to camp. I went straight to bed and had no problem falling asleep.

August 18, 1989, Friday

The filming of the fight scenes was supposed to have been complete on Thursday; but the film crew was behind and kept everyone who wanted to stay on for Friday. Six Confederates had to leave, among them was Paul Williams, a member of The Straight Eight.

We went through the same routine as on previous days. Doc had left again. This time he went up to the Houck Buffalo Ranch to help pitch tents for the Ft. Sedwick scene. So I was back to being a member of The Straight Eight. The crew filmed more of the same shots as before. This time Kevin did all of his own riding across the field and along the Confederate line. The crew filmed the whole sequence from beginning to end.

Frank's double was bad on Frank's horse. During one filming sequence, he almost ran over some of the reenactors. Frank's horse always had great explosions of gas when he started to run. We made Frank's horse the official mascot of the Royal Order of Raccoons.

The wind and dust for the past few days had been terrible by even South Dakota standards. We attempted various ways to protect our food and drink from blowing dirt (which was also probably part horse and cow manure); but whatever we tried, the dirt still got into the food.

Tim, Bruce, and I had a chance to talk with Michael Blake, the author of *Dances With Wolves*. He said it took eight months to write the book.

HATZELL
. 1989
CONFEDERATE TROOPS
RENDERED EARLY FRIDAY
AUGUST 18, 1989

WHILE WAITING FOR
MAKEUP CALL WHILE ON
SET OF "DANCES WITH
WOLVES"

He wrote it when he was between jobs and living out of his car. The Costners invited him to their house for showers during that time period.

The afternoon was filled with specialty shots. Some Confederates were put in a prisoner of war scene. Those of us who were not in the scene were herded off the set.

One bone of contention was the capture of the Confederate flags. Kevin wanted the Union troops to capture the flags. Some of the Confederate reenactors were adamant the Confederate colors not be taken, but that they escape. Kevin finally relented.

Back on the Confederate line, Frank's horse dropped a pile of green road apples. One of the older men started kicking them at a sixteen year old kid. He pleaded with the man to stop; but the more he asked him to stop, the more the man went after him. I walked over to the green horse turds, picked one up, and threw it at the man. It hit him on the hand and pants. He stopped. "See, it's nothing. Just fight fire with fire!" I said.

The afternoon continued with specialty scenes including people being shot or running through the cornfield while being chased by cavalry. Jason was filmed running through the cornfield. He did a good job.

The film crew had filled a ravine with water halfway up to the knee. The crew wanted two Confederates to run up the stream bed and three more Confederates to run down the side of the ravine into the stream bed. When they all got together, they were to scramble through the mud and up the other side. All the while, two saber wielding Union cavalry soldiers on horses would be chasing them.

The film crew wanted volunteers.

I'm thirty-eight years old. I have a bad knee and didn't bring my knee brace along. What the heck—how many times do you get to be in a movie? I thought. So I volunteered.

I was to be one of the three to run down the side of the ravine. The leather soles of my shoes were very slippery. An older reenactor told me to get them muddy, that would give me extra traction.

The film crew told each of us when to run. I was to be number 2. I did not want to take my Enfield musket down through the mud and water, so they gave me a rubber musket.

"1 go!", the director shouted. "2 go! 3 go!"

I ran fast—almost straight down and sloshed through the water. I moved as fast as I could and dared not look behind me. The bank we had to scramble up seemed almost straight up. I had no idea how close the horses were. My bummer flew off my head. I made a feeble attempt to get it and left it behind. We all made it to the top and outran the horses before the film crew yelled "Cut!"

"Beautiful! Wonderful!" the director said. "Do it again."

I was breathing hard and my chest was heaving. "If it was beautiful and wonderful," I gasped, "why do we have to do it again?"

"Why—we do everything twice in Hollywood." the director answered.

We slid back down the bank, sloshed through the water, and pulled ourselves back up to the starting position. I was still out of breath.

"Those horses weren't moving fast enough. Speed them up this time!" the lead cameraman said.

"Hey!" I shouted "I'm gonna be moving a lot slower than the first time!"

"Just run like they are going to slash you with those swords," he answered.

I'm going to run as if their horses are going to trample me! I thought.

We went through the whole sequence again, my heart pounding in my chest. I got through the water all right; but slipped in the mud as I tried to scramble up the slippery, muddy slope. I could hear the horses coming up behind us and with an extra special effort scrambled upward. My bummer flew off my head. The horses trampled it. But again I got away.

The director liked the scene this time so we did not have to do it again.

"Give each of them an extra twenty-five dollars," he told Dave Silva. I was full of mud; but felt elated.

The crew filmed a few more specialty shots. Two stunt men had a fight scene in the water. We were told to gather our gear and walk (not march) over to the Union side. A group of us ran out to a fake dead Holstein and had our picture taken with it as one of those hunter trophy scenes, with the Confederate flag flying in the back.

There was one last scene of Yankees walking captured rebels through a large cornfield. Kevin wanted the Union soldiers to carry the Confederates' muskets. Bill Blake politely told him that during the Civil War, the captors let prisoners carry their muskets; but with the butt end up in the air. Kevin thought about it and let them do it that way. The film crew liked how the picture looked.

After picking up my extra twenty-five dollars for the run and a short meeting at the mess tent where we were told they really liked the work we had done, we walked back up to our camp and were given our checks for the work we had done up to that point in time.

Most people were leaving after today's filming. Thirty-eight reenactors would be staying for Saturday's hospital scene.

A thunderstorm was brewing in the West. Large streaks of lightning zigzagged above the horizon.

I had offered Don and Bill rides to town. I helped them pack their gear, beat the storm to town, and got them situated in the Kings Inn. I went home to see Liz and the kids. I took a bath, got something to eat, and drove back out to De Grey.

That reminds me of a story Don told about De Grey. When Don came to South Dakota, he rode to the set in a film crew van. The driver had never been to the set and had been told to head east on Highway 34 until he saw the De Grey sign and take a left. The driver thought the person said "The gray sign". They had passed the De Grey sign when he realized the mistake.

Quick
Sketch

Rendered on the hospital set of
the film "Dances with Wolves"
Saturday morning August 19, 1989

Simon Danoff

When I got back out to the site, the security guard gave me a ride out to the camp. It was a cool night and I fell asleep right away.

August 19, 1989, Saturday

I am not sure what time we got up; but it was later than 5:30 a.m. Today I was to be a Yankee, so I put on the blue uniform. We were going to do the hospital scene so I did not need my musket. We did not march to breakfast; but had a leisurely walk. There were about thirty-eight reenactors. I was the only one remaining from the Pierre group, and Terry had left.

After eating, we formed up into ranks and marched to makeup and then marched back up to the hospital set. The film crew placed people in various positions to do things while the cameras would be rolling. Some stood around the dinner table, one was a cook, others were to lie in the beds as sick soldiers.

I was selected to sit at a table outside a tent and play chess with a soldier named Steve from Montana. He had been an extra on several different TV shows—I had never heard of any of them. He was friends with Andy Cannon and said Andy would be putting together extras for a movie this winter in Montana based on Jack London's book *White Fang*. That sounded like it would be fun.

Steve Morris from Pierre was in this scene. He lost a leg when he was sixteen in a motorcycle accident. Steve took off his artificial leg. The set people bandaged it to make it look as if it had just been cut off. He was to stand with a crutch while watching our chess game.

Montana Steve's queen was missing so we replaced it with a chunk of wood. I wanted to play a real game of chess. So it started out as a real game; but after several moves Montana Steve wanted to use some fake moves. Maybe I was beating him.

It started to get hot as the day wore on. The crew filmed several scenes from the hospital tent Kevin would be in. Montana Steve was sure we would be on camera because Kevin gave a lot of direction to Steve Morris as to where to stand and when to turn to take a cup of coffee from Jim Hatzell.

Jim was a western artist from Rapid City, South Dakota. He was always working in his sketchbook during downtime. I introduced myself and asked if I could see his sketches. I thought they were very good as I flipped the pages. Jim sketched a little girl and gave her the finished product. Later Cindy Costner walked over to Jim and asked if he was the one who had sketched the little girl. He let her look through his sketchbook. She liked it.

During the hospital scene, Dunbar sees Steve has lost a leg and decides he does not want his foot cut off so he runs away. Kevin worked closely with us during a large part of the morning. After finishing a variety of scenes including the two doctors leaving the hospital tent for a cup of coffee, we broke for lunch.

It was a good pleasant lunch—no wind and few flies. The crew and reenactors walked back to the set after eating.

Bill Costner was talking with Steve Morris and me. I saw Kevin was allowing people to take pictures with him. Bill told us to run over and get our pictures taken with his son; but just as he said it, Kevin started to turn away. Thinking quickly, I asked Bill if he would ask his son to come over and have his picture taken with us since Steve could not move too fast with one leg. "Sure," he said and brought over Kevin. I handed Bill my camera and he took the picture. From out of nowhere Mike O'Connell, a kid with the Irish Battalion, jumped into the picture with us. We thanked the Costners and went back to work.

The film crew did not use me in any scenes for the rest of the day; but people who were in the "line of sight" from the tent had to stand by on reserve if needed for later shots.

Rumor had it the third biggest film producer in the United States was there to watch the filming. This man and his wife had been involved

Quick
Sketches

HATZELL
1989

BILL COSTNER
RENDERED AT JAMAICAN POOL PARTY
PIERRE, SOUTH DAKOTA
SATURDAY EVENING AUGUST 19, 1989

with *Star Wars* and never visited movie sets; but they had made an exception for this.

Most of the afternoon scenes were of Dunbar seeing his mangled foot and then pulling on the boot. They must have filmed the same scene over and over again at least twenty times. It became boring, as we had to stay quiet while listening to Kevin's moans and screams.

Between filming, I was sitting cross-legged on the ground ripping up blades of grass one at a time. A man walked up and stood over me.

"Aren't you Bill Markley?" he said.

"Yes."

He was Bill Stevens whom I had known from my early years in state government. He was working for the movie as a production assistant and driver. Bill had just bought a video camera and had permission to record the behind the scenes action.

The people who were not in the line of sight got to film some additional battle scenes; I almost wished I could have been with them.

At one point filming had to stop until a low flying plane left the area. The sound equipment could pick up the noise.

It was about 6:00 p.m. when the crew filmed Dunbar's escape from the hospital. They drove a film truck beside him and filmed as he galloped away from camp. They filmed this three times and then we were done.

The continuous sound of musket fire came from the battlefield set. I put on my gear, picked up my musket, and walked down there to see if I could get in on the action.

I ran into Bill, the cameraman, and asked if they needed me. He said I was perfect for a small scene of bored soldiers; but when I told him I had been one of the chess players, he did not want to use me because I might be recognized. They did use my blanket.

When the filming was over, I walked back to the parking area and picked up my paycheck from Andy Cannon and let him know I was available for the Ft. Sedgewick scenes if they needed me. Andy said he might have a few openings and would call me. I drove up to the hospital set, loaded my gear, and helped take down some of the tents that would not be needed for the night.

Tonight the production company was holding a cast party for the reenactors. I was taking Liz. Helen was going to watch the kids for the night.

I gave Bill, Doc, and Mike a ride to town and dropped them off at the YMCA for showers. It was 8:30 p.m. by the time I got home.

I took a quick bath and grabbed something to eat. Liz and I rushed off to the cast party that was being held at the city pool at Griffith Park. The party was a Jamaican luau, a combination Jamaican-Hawaiian theme. We were to wear Hawaiian clothing and everyone received a plastic lei when they entered the pool area. Someone had made large cut-out palm trees. Loud Jamaican and rock music played over a music system.

I was surprised to see Terry and Cindy Pool. Terry had talked Cindy into staying for the party. The Huxfords, Larsons, and Engelmanns were there. The crowd grew as the night rolled on. There were plenty of food, beer, and mixed drinks. One crew member wore a long black-hair wig and continuously walked around with a tray of mixed drinks, handing them out to all in need.

Kevin and Cindy Costner as well as his parents, Bill and Sharon mingled with the crowd. Kevin joined our small group of reenactors. I introduced myself and shook his hand. Then I yelled to Liz to join us and introduced her to Kevin.

"Part of the deal for allowing me to be in the movie was so Liz could meet you!"

"You guys did a great job," he said as he patted me on the back. I told him I was in the ravine scene. Kevin liked that scene and hoped it did not wind up on the cutting room floor. I told him I enjoyed working on the movie and thanked him for the opportunity.

People were loosening up and dancing. Every now and then someone would give the Royal Order of Raccoon hand signal. We tried to get Kevin to join the lodge again; but he again said "I think you guys have to be a little more selective."

The Limbo song started to play. People stood in line to do the limbo. I decided against it because of my bad knee. Liz persuaded Clyde Kocher to get Kevin's signature for her on a napkin. It read "Liz, see you at the movies! Love Kevin."

One of the many songs played was the "Banana Boat Song" from the *Beetlejuice* movie soundtrack. Several of the film crew had worked on that movie. One of the makeup people told us he had done the special effects masks and makeup.

The crowd did a line dance around the swimming pool to the "Banana Boat Song". Kevin and Cindy Costner continued to mingle and dance with the group.

Liz and I talked with Bill the cameraman and his wife.

"You guys were great!" he said. "It was hilarious. There we were on one side of the fence with all our cameras taking your pictures. When we were done, then you would all pull out your cameras and take our pictures. It was like a battle!"

A good time was had by all. Cindy Costner helped the crew pick up trash after the party. We left at 2:30 a.m. and went to the Happy Chef Restaurant for breakfast. Cindy Costner and one of the crewmen came in after cleaning up and ate a large order of french fries. We got to bed about 4:00 a.m.

CHAPTER 4 BETWEEN TIMES

◆

August 20, 1989, Sunday

We slept in late, missing church. Bill Stevens invited Liz and me down to the softball fields to watch the film crew play Sunday night softball. Sometimes Kevin is there—this evening he was not.

August 21, 1989, Monday

Back to the old grind at work. I was bone tired and depressed. Andy Cannon had said he had some openings for the Ft. Sedgewick set. I had let him know I was available for work on the set; but he did not call.

August 24, 1989, Thursday

After work I called Jack Hangar at his motel room. I wanted to return the uniform that I had had dry cleaned and accouterments I had borrowed. He was interested in seeing the pictures I had taken on the set. He said to come down to the Ramkota Motel where they were going to watch the dailies. The dailies were film clips shot earlier, developed, and sent back for viewing. Jack said anybody could come in to watch them.

After Liz got home from work I drove down to the motel. The dailies were in progress. The room was dark and packed with people. I found a seat on the floor.

The dailies were from the field hospital scenes. The first film clips were shots of the camp from inside the tent. It would have been Lieutenant Dunbar's point of view. I could just barely see myself playing chess. Then they had the close-up of Steve Morris's leg. He was standing in front of me. You could see everything of me; but my face! So much for stardom.

There were lots of shots of Kevin pulling on his boot and screaming in pain. During one shot, he had a blank look on his face.

"I forget what I'm supposed to do!" he said. The crowd roared with laughter. Kevin took it good-naturedly. They showed the escape scenes and that was it.

Kevin Costner came up to Jim Hatzell. "You're the guy that sketches, let me see." Jim handed him his sketchbook. "Pretty good!" he said as he flipped the pages.

Jack, Clyde, and Frank had not eaten supper so we walked over to the Town and Country Restaurant and sat down at a table with Kevin Costner's parents. We had an enjoyable conversation with them. They were retired and were enjoying every minute of it. They were going to spend some time in the Black Hills. I suggested they drive to Rochford to see some unspoiled back country.

The others headed to the Longbranch Saloon. I went home.

August 29, 1989, Tuesday

Liz's good friend, Kathy Olson, sat at our dining room table with Liz and me, looking at *Dances With Wolves* photographs. We were discussing how depressed everyone was after the filming had finished. We all agreed we wished it could continue.

The telephone rang. It was Jack Hangar. He wanted to know if I wanted to be back in the movie! Filming would be from September 13 to16 outside of Rapid City. The scenes would be of Ft. Hays when Dunbar leaves for Ft. Sedgewick. Of course I said yes.

To make a long story short, Dale, Bruce, Tim and I were all back in the film. Some of them initially said no; but as time went on they thought it over and changed their calendars of events to hit the movie trail again.

September 1, 1989, Friday

Terry called and said he had made arrangements for our uniforms. He will not be able to make this round of filming.

September 4, 1989, Monday, Labor Day

Liz came home from work at 3:30 p.m. She had had a busy day. We picked up Bob and Nancy Shoup and their kids and drove down to De Grey to show them the movie set.

Things had really changed. No one was there. All tents, vehicles, and equipment were gone. Most of the rail fence was gone except for a few sections in front of the house. The house was still standing; but the fake brick had been removed from the chimneys. The shed was still there and the outhouse. The ravine I had sloshed through was now bone dry. The large stump I had stood near while on the Confederate line was still there. The spray paint was still on the leaves. We picked up silk leaves and plastic ivy on the ground then drove over to the abandoned hospital set and home. I called Jack Hangar. He gave me an update—the filming start date was changed to September 14.

CHAPTER 5 FRONTIER

◆

September 14, 1989, Thursday

Bruce Huxford, Tim Larson, Dale Englemann and I had been invited back to work as extras on the *Dances With Wolves* Ft. Hays set. We were to portray dismounted federal cavalry soldiers at Ft. Hays, a frontier post that the film company built near Caputa, southeast of Rapid City, South Dakota. We were to meet Jack Hanger at the set. He would have uniforms for us to borrow.

I got up at 6:30 a.m., ate breakfast and finished packing my GMC Jimmy. After saying goodbye to Liz and the kids, I drove across the Missouri River bridge to Ft. Pierre and picked up Dale at his house. We followed Bruce and Tim in Bruce's van. We drove out across the prairie on Highway 14 to Interstate 90 heading west on the Interstate to New Underwood. We then traveled south and west on Highway 44 until we reached the small town of Caputa. We followed the unpaved road south of Caputa for two miles until we reached the gate to the Ft. Hays movie set.

The Black Hills were on the western horizon. Mt. Rushmore was just barely visible.

Campers, horse trailers, and modern tents lined the north fence line. Teepees and Civil War era wall tents were grouped to the southwest with vehicles parked behind them. Some of the teepees had what looked like scalps dangling from the lodge pole tops. B-1 Bombers flew overhead. The Air Force would reroute them once the movie started.

The camp was alive with people on horseback; dogs ran everywhere; men, women and children were busy with all kinds of activities. Only a few women and children had been at the Civil War set.

We stepped into Andy Cannon's trailer to check in; but found out we could not do so without our papers. Jack was in Rapid City and had left our papers with old Harry Thoad. Harry had been with the Irish Battalion on the Civil War movie set. Harry was nowhere to be found.

Skip Harrington and Joe Acamo also with the Irish Battalion drove into camp from Nebraska. They had been Confederate cavalry during the Civil War scenes and had seen little action. We visited with them. I ran into Paul Williams who had brought his horse, Shiloh, and would be portraying a mounted cavalry trooper.

Bruce had his pop-up trailer at Hart Ranch, a tourist resort in the Black Hills, and was going to bring it to the movie campsite to use. Tim and I rode with him to bring it back while Dale remained in camp to track down Harry and our papers. Bruce hauled the trailer back to the campsite and we helped him set it up.

We finally found Harry smoking a pipe clenched between his few remaining teeth. He gave us our papers and we checked in at Andy's camper.

Since Bruce's trailer had three beds and there were four of us, I set up my six-man tent for myself so "I can live like a desert sheik!"

Bob Erickson, a cavalry reenactor from Montana and assistant to Andy Cannon, told us "Be in uniform by 3 o'clock at the mess tent. People with horses need to be mounted."

The reenactors gathered at the mess tent at 3:00 p.m. It was hot and dusty. Everyone looked authentic, especially the mountain men and women who looked like they were dressed in their finest for one of the annual fur trading rendezvous of the early nineteenth century. Most of them wore buckskin with beadwork and fringe. Their heads were covered with a variety headgear ranging from broad-brimmed hats to animal skins. One man wore a double-skunkskin cap.

Andy Cannon held a short informational meeting to give us the set rules. Reveille was at 5:00 a.m. Breakfast was at 6:00 a.m. The wardrobe people gave us the once-over to make sure our clothing was correct for the time period. Most of the soldiers passed inspection; but the buckskinners were told to tone down their clothes. Wardrobe wanted them to look plain since they were to portray buffalo hunters.

The mounted cavalry ran through a series of drills. Andy dismissed those of us on foot. I wandered into the sutler's tent. A sutler was a storekeeper who followed the army to sell the soldiers items not normally provided by the army. J.D., the sutler, and his wife had various reenacting supplies and items of interest for sale. A display case contained Bowie knives and an Arkansas Toothpick modeled after the pirate Jean Laffite's knife in a New Orleans museum. J.D. showed me an Apache arrowhead. "See how it's curved so when it hits a bone, it slips off and continues deeper into the flesh. It's designed so it can't be pulled out backwards but has to be pushed all the way through the other side." I bought a pair of lead dice made from minie balls.

As I came out of the sutler's tent, I ran into Jim Hatzell. He wore a dark blue vest and stripped shirt, on his head was a broad-brimmed hat; and he carried a Henry rifle.

"I must be a buffalo hide buyer since I'm dressed so nice," Jim joked.

Our neighbor to the North of Bruce's camper was Allen, a buckskinner from Waubay Lakes, South Dakota. He pronounced "Allen" by putting the emphasis on the *A*. He was staying in a small tent. My tent was on the right at the end of a long line of tents. To the left of Allen tented Mike Terry who was portraying an Indian scout. To his left were Dave and Dan Baumann, brothers from Colorado. They had been on the Civil War set. Dave was one of The Straight Eight. Dan had been on the Union side. Next in line on the left was Paul Williams who would be sleeping in his horse trailer. Next to him was Clyde and Jack's horse trailer. They were not here; they were staying in a Rapid City motel. There were others farther down the line, but I did not know them.

Bruce made a pot of chili. We invited Allen to eat with us and drink a few beers. Dave and Dan stopped over for a beer and brought their photographs from the Civil War set. I dug mine out and we sat in the twilight looking at pictures until we could not make them out anymore.

Dan told us when he and Dave were younger they had been badly hurt by a cannon. They were loading the cannon during a reenactment. It went off prematurely. Dan's hand was severely damaged. Dave was also badly hurt. They were in a remote area of the Colorado mountains, so a helicopter had to fly them out to a hospital. They made complete recoveries; but Dan's little finger could not be straightened.

Loud singing and laughter came from the buckskinners' teepees.

"Let's mosey on down and see what the Leather Underwear Boys are up to," Bruce said.

We walked over to see what was happening. The full moon rose in the East so bright, it almost appeared to be daylight.

A good campfire blazed in front of a lean-to shelter between two teepees. Cast iron pots and kettles hung over the flames. Eight people sat around the fire. The six men were dressed in mountain man garb. The two women wore modern clothes. One of the men strummed a guitar while he sang an old fur trapping song. They invited us to join them by the fire.

I sat on a wooden chest next to Marla. Her jovial husband, Tim Teegerstrom sat on the other side of the fire. He looked as if he had just walked in from trapping beaver. He had long sandy colored hair and beard and wore a leather fringed shirt and leggings.

The guitar player's name was Blue Hawk and his wife's name was Belinda. There was Rick, Terry, Elder Sheets who wore the two-skunk-skins cap, and Rabi.

Rabi had a long full beard and hair, He wore little wire-rim glasses and a broad brimmed hat with a turkey feather dangling behind. He told me how he got his name. He was attending his first mountain man rendezvous. He was hunched over a small fire cooking a piece of meat on a stick.

"He looks like a rabbi," someone said and the name stuck.

It was easy to let my mind drift and imagine what it must have been like one-hundred-fifty years ago when the fur trade was in full bloom.

The old songs were fun to listen to. Blue Hawk would explain the background of a song, try to teach us the chorus, and we would attempt to sing along at the top of our lungs. Some were serious, some were funny; but most were bawdy. The fire crackled. In between songs, the merry band exchanged jokes and stories.

Coyotes howled out on the far ridges setting the dogs to barking and howling in response.

We performed a mass induction of the buckskinners into the Royal Order of Raccoons. They were happy to become members.

It was getting cold. By 9:30 p.m., the group broke up. I was in my sleeping bag on top of the cot by 10:15 p.m. It had been a good day.

September 15, 1989, Friday

Animals rummaging through the trash bag outside the tent woke me up during the middle of the night. The aroma of skunk was in the air. It was very cold and I did not want to get out of my warm sleeping bag to investigate.

It seemed as if I had no sooner fallen off to sleep than I was awakened by someone walking past the tent and relieving himself. I quickly jumped out of the bag and poked my head out of the tent to see Dale walking back to the camper. He was fully dressed in his uniform.

It was still night. The full moon shone in the western sky. The light was on in the camper and I could hear people moving around inside.

"Dale what time is it?"

"Twenty minutes to six."

I slept right through reveille! I thought.

I quickly dressed in my Union Civil War uniform and hurried over to the camper. Bruce was boiling water for coffee. Tim was lying on his bunk half dressed and crabby. Dale was looking sheepish, not saying anything.

Bruce told me what was going on. Dale had set his watch alarm for 5:00 a.m. It went off and everyone got up. Bruce walked down the line of tents and trailers to use a port-a-potty and noticed no one else was out and about yet. He looked at his watch and it was not even close to 5:00 a.m. Dale had his watch set for Central Time. We were on Mountain Time, so we were up an hour before we needed to be.

There we were, awake, dressed, and drinking coffee before the 5:00 a.m. reveille. We gave Dale a good-natured hard-time for the rest of the day; he took it well.

After reveille, we had an hour until breakfast. It was still dark when we had breakfast under the mess tent. The caterer had a large truck in which meals were cooked. The loud hum of the electric generators was constant. The food was good and the coffee steaming hot.

What a motley crew we were—soldiers, mountain men, and women. Horses were in the background near the tent. The ever present dogs chased each other. They looked at you with sad eyes, hoping for scraps off your plate.

The sky started to lighten in the East. The cavalry mounted up and rode off to the set. Those of us without horses climbed into vans for the ride to Base Camp.

The sun came up five minutes after the full moon set in the West. I thought of Genesis, "And God made the Sun to rule the day and the Moon to rule the night."

It was about a half mile drive to Base Camp where the set production trailers were located. We passed a reconstructed sod hut. We speculated this was the set for the scene where the Sioux rescue the little girl, Stands With a Fist, from the Pawnee.

The van dropped us off at Base Camp, a collection of trucks, trailers, and vans that contained the major actors' dressing rooms, props, wardrobe, makeup, caterer, and a variety of other purposes.

I grabbed a cup of hot coffee from the caterer van and tried to warm up in the weak rays of the new day's sun.

HATZELL
1980?

Carol
Sloggett
Rendezvous at Ferry Hayes
Film Site of Motion Picture
"Dances with Wolves"
Friday September 15, 1989   South Dakota

Wardrobe checked us over to make sure we looked right. They decided we did not need makeup. We went to the props truck where we were given waist-belts, cartridge boxes, cap pouches, pistol holsters, and pistols. Props handed me a rubber pistol.

We had two and a half hours to kill—lots of conversation. We started getting punchy. I forget what I said but after I said it Bruce was telling everyone "Don't give Markley anything sharp! He might hurt himself."

Finally, the vans returned to take us to the Ft. Hays set, about a half mile farther on from Base Camp. What a great set. A large parade ground with a flagpole in the middle dominated the set. Along the east side was a buffalo hunter's camp, complete with hides, skulls, and other bones. Next in line was a barber shop and bath house, then a trading post with all kinds of pots, pans, furs, cloth, knives, pipes, beads, etc. After that there was a working sawmill with an original old-time steam-powered saw. Next was the supply depot at the north end of the parade ground. To its left was the headquarters building, very impressive. The brick and the tops of the chimneys were blackened to make it look as if there had been a lot of use. Behind the depot was a blacksmith shop and corral with horses, mules, and longhorn cattle. On the west side of the parade ground were three rows of tents in front of which were shelters for cooking food and dining tables.

The buffalo hunters, women, and a few soldiers including Tim and Dale were to remain on the barber shop side of the parade ground. Eight of us were told to cross over to the cooking and eating area. The soldiers on horses were forming up to do their drills. The kitchen and mess area were interesting. Stuffed deer hung from the crossbeams of the bough covered shelter or "cooler." Turkeys, quail, and a stringer of fresh fish were hanging. Pens held live rabbits and chickens. The tables were filled with 1860's era pots, pans, and utensils, piles of onions, potatoes, and corn. We were not to move anything from its original position.

Not a cloud was in the sky as it started to get warm. We sat in the shade and waited. The cavalry looked good as they rode past. The sounds were of hoof beats, rattling sabers, occasional orders, and horse whinnies.

Linda Brachman, the assistant director, began to position us as the film crew set up cameras at the end of the tents. Bruce was to cut onions. Others were to sit and talk or lounge. Brodie, who was from California, and I were to walk across the parade ground to the bathhouse for a bath and shave. During this scene, everyone is busy doing something as Dunbar rides into the fort.

At the last minute, Linda pulled me from walking across the parade ground. She wanted four of us to pour buckets of water into the water trough. The film crew set up the camera alongside the water trough. I was the second person from the camera. Linda told me "After you pour the water out of the bucket, dip your hand in the trough and splash water on your face." Kevin directed this close-up scene. I was nervous.

"Background!"

"Action!"

We walked up to the trough, poured in the water, and stepped back. Rod Ferry with the Irish Battalion and three others brought eight horses to the water trough. The scene appeared to run great until the film crew reviewed the film and saw that the water being poured out of the first bucket was red! The bucket had held fake blood earlier and had not been cleaned out. The whole scene was wrecked and had to be shot again. Kevin was not happy.

During this scene, Mike O'Connell was to sell chickens to one of the buffalo hunters. Mike had never held a chicken before and asked Linda to show him how to do it!

On the other side of the parade ground, Tim was at the bathhouse waiting for a shave. Dale walked out of the trading post and onto the parade ground.

HOTZELL
1989

Quick
Sketch

KEVIN COSTNER

ON THE SHOT MAKER

RIDING FRIDAY AFTERNOON
SEPTEMBER 29, 1989

The film crew shot this same scene a variety of times from various angles using different lenses. One shot had to be redone because a fly got into the lens of a camera. It was now very hot. Craft Services had water and lemonade available in one of the tents. I got some for the horse-holders and myself. I relieved Rod Ferry and held his horse. Kevin was up close to us. His parents were there and talked with me.

The next scene was farther down the line as Dunbar rides up to the Headquarters building. Linda had us sit at a table and pretend to eat. Mike O'Connell was to my left. Two Minnesotans sat across the table. The one directly across from me was Jack Kolledge. Jack was with the 1st Minnesota and had portrayed a Union soldier during the Civil War scenes.

After several shots of this scene, we boarded the vans that took us back to camp for lunch. It was good food and more than we could eat. The film company threw out all leftover food.

Back on the set, Linda told us to take the same positions we had before lunch. This time the crew filmed us so close, they put real stew on our plates and dry ice in the pitcher to make it look like steaming coffee. I was the only one who trusted eating the stew. The beef was not bad. I must have been eating out of habit since my stomach was already full. My back was to the camera in this scene.

We had another long wait until the next scene. Dan told us about The Balloonatics. During the Civil War scenes on the Union side, he and a few others were to stay around the observation balloon that the Confederates had shot down. They were in very little filming so to entertain themselves, they did a lot of crazy things and gave themselves the name The Balloonatics.

During the set up of one of the scenes, I walked up onto the porch of the Headquarters building to look around. Maury Chaykin who played the suicidal Major sat in a chair on the front porch. He was a large man, balding in front with long greasy hair (makeup made all our hair look greasy). I introduced myself and tried to talk with him; but he was not in a talkative mood. He must have been trying to get into character for his upcoming scenes.

The film crew started to set up for the scene where Dunbar would ride out of the fort with the teamster Timmons. The wagon was along the back of the supply depot across from the headquarters building. Linda positioned everyone at the loading dock except for Dan and me. She told us to go to the backside of the wagon. We thought we would be in the background. Wrong—we were in the foreground!

We were to load the wagon and tie down the load with ropes. Timmons played by Robert Pastorelli yells at us and gives us a hard time. Dan does not do much and soon disappears. A blond-haired kid brings out a string of cups. Timmons yells at him and jerks the cups out of his hand. I was told to lash a surveying tripod to the side of the wagon. I carry it onto the scene. "Argue with Timmons; but do as he says," I was told. After the blond-haired kid gets it, Timmons turns to me.

I am starting to tie the tripod to the side of the wagon. He grabs a loose chain hanging from the wagon.

"What's this?" he yells. "Tie it up! Tie it up!"

"Do it yourself!" I grumble.

He walks toward me shouting "Hey Muttonhead! You do it! You do it!"

I say a few more words in protest and start tying up the tripod with the chain. He is shouting at me the whole time. Someone yelled "Cut!"

Robert put his arm around my shoulder. "Hey what's your name?"

"Bill."

"Bill, I hope you realize I don't mean anything by it."

"Oh sure, I understand."

It was scary knowing Kevin and the whole production crew were watching my every move. We did this scene three times. On one of the takes, Timmons yelled at me to put the tripod on top of the wagon instead of on the side. I gave him a hard time about that. We got into a good argument; but I did what he said. The production people liked it.

It was very hot and dusty. My friends had to continually haul and stack boxes in the background as this scene was being filmed. This made the third time today I was in a close up scene and my friends were getting suspicious.

"Markley how much did you have to pay to be put up close to the cameras?" Bruce accused.

The mules were hitched to the wagon and pulled it away. The next scene was the Major shooting himself in the head. Linda placed me on the loading dock with the others carrying cartridge boxes from one pile and stacking them on another pile. Linda would shout "Bang!" and then we would run to the window of the Major's office and look in. We did this scene again and again until it was sunset and the film crew called it a day.

It was dark by the time we got back to camp. The full moon was on the rise to the East as the mounted troops and civilians rode into camp. Rod hurt his groin as he trotted his horse. Mike borrowed Clyde's horse to ride back to camp. The horse stepped in a prairie dog hole and then bucked him off.

Bruce, Tim, Dale, and I drove to Hart Ranch to take showers. It felt good to get cleaned up.

We stopped at a convenience store to pick up beer and call home. Everyone at home was doing fine. Some of the buckskinners came in to buy beer dressed in their buckskins. People sure did give them a second look.

Back at camp, Bruce made supper. We invited Allen who brought his beef mixed with pork. It was very good.

After washing dishes, we walked down to the buckskinner's campfire. The full moon was so bright we did not need flashlights and did not have to worry about stepping in prairie dog holes.

Blue Hawk and Belinda had gone to bed so there was no singing. We sat around the fire and told stories and jokes.

HATZELL
1989

Quick
Sketch
painters on the set
of the motion picture "Dances with Wolves"
Thursday afternoon
September 14, 1989
South Dakota

One of the older long-haired, long-bearded mountain men was Dennis Des Jardins. He wore a long buffalo robe coat that was over one hundred years old. The hair was worn off the coat where the wearer sat down. Dennis and his wife, Maria, were from Montana. He claimed this was the first time he had crossed back east of the Rockies in the last twenty years. Dennis went to his teepee and returned with a jug to pass around.

"What is it?" I asked as he uncorked the jug and handed it to me.

"Montana Whistle or Apple Pie."

All eyes were on me. No one spoke. The only sound was the crackling fire.

I had experienced backwoods moonshine during my college fraternity days at the Virginia Tech DKE house. I braced myself as I got ready to take a swig. I expected to taste something awful that would instantly rip off the back of my head. But a wonderful flavor entered my mouth and flowed down my throat.

"Oh Boy!" I emphatically exclaimed and quickly took another longer pull on the jug. The campfire crowd roared with laughter.

"You sound like a kid in a candy store," Bruce said. Everyone had to sample the jug after that. There were plenty of "Oh Boy!" jokes for the rest of the night.

The Northern Lights shimmered in the clear sky.

Dennis was proud of his Scottish heritage. He went into his teepee and brought out a steel Claymore broad sword he had made. Dennis was feeling no pain from the Montana Whistle. Hefting the monstrous gleaming blade with both hands over his head, he swung it around in large arcs. Everyone made sure to stand far away from him.

The coyotes sang to the full moon as the temperature dropped. I was snug in my warm sleeping bag by 1:00 a.m. and fell asleep immediately.

September 16, 1989, Saturday

The bugle sounded at 5:00 a.m. It was so cold, I did not want to get out of my sleeping bag. I pulled my clothes into the bag to warm them up before I dressed. It was still cold and dark when we ate a good breakfast of eggs, sausage, and plenty of hot steaming coffee.

We were bussed back out to Base Camp. The van hit a large bump on the road. A woman sitting behind me had been drinking coffee. The hot coffee flew out of her cup and down my back. She was very sorry; but I made light of it.

At Base Camp I turned in the Enfield musket I had been given. Cavalry did not use Enfield rifles but used Sharps carbines. A sign by one of the coffee pots read "For Background Artists Only". After that, we started calling ourselves Background Artists.

Tim, Bruce, and the others gave me a hard time about being in all the close-up shots. They elected me "President of the Background Artists Union."

We were taken back out to the set and had time to kill. We began thinking of making our own video called "Major Lee Depressed" named after the Major who blows his brains out. We had tryouts for the Major and took pictures of ourselves pretending to shoot each other—all at the same time.

After tiring of "Major Lee Depressed" try-outs, we sat at the tables in the shade of the coolers. Dale was riding today since Rod had hurt himself yesterday. They selected several of us for inside the Headquarters shots. The group was narrowed down to Tim, Dale, Rod, Dan, and Brodie. Andy Cannon told them to wait for a few minutes in the middle of the drill field. We named them The Bureaucrat Brigade. A short wait turned into an hour under the broiling sun. Andy returned and told them to wait in the shade with the rest of us.

The bathhouse women were bored and walked across the parade ground to visit us. We ended up taking silly pictures with them. We posed two of them sitting on Tim and Bruce's laps and had everyone else gather around. Our photographer yelled "Look like you just returned from months on the prairie!"

The film crew called for The Bureaucrat Brigade after what seemed like forever. They went into the Headquarters building. Kevin and his staff looked them over. Kevin selected two for the inside shots—Tim and Dan. They sent the others back. The film crew wanted two clean shaven people who had the same hair color as Kevin so they did not stand out. What great luck for Tim and Dan. The makeup people slicked back their hair and then sat them at two desks in the front room. When Dunbar walks into the room, they look up and when he asks for the Major, they nod their heads toward his office. They shot this scene a variety of times with different lenses and angles.

"You'll be on the silver screen—bigger than life!" I later said to Tim.

Meanwhile the film crew placed the rest of us back at the mess tables. I sat on the right end of the table, facing the Headquarters building. Mike sat to my left, then Joe Acamo. Across from me sat Jack Kollodge and Gene who was a founding member of the 1st Minnesota. Jack told me the 1st Minnesota was one of the first reenactor groups in the country to do everything by the book, making sure their clothing and equipment was of the proper period.

We had plenty of time to wait. Jack and I held extensive conversations on a variety of topics that included reenacting, genealogy, what our ancestors did in the Civil War, and the Grand Army of the Republic. Jack collects GAR memorabilia.

The film crew shot the eating scene several times. Gene and Joe stood up from the table and left to wash their plates. Jack got up and brought back a pot of coffee and poured me a cup. Of course we were faking the eating and drinking. These will be background scenes filmed from inside the Headquarters.

The wind came up and blew strong. We broke for lunch after 1:00 p.m. and had grilled steak. It was great!

Back at the set, I ran into Bill Stevens who was doing a variety of jobs for Kevin Costner. We visited for a few minutes. He was going to try to get his family on the set.

The next scene was Dunbar leading his horse to the wagon while the Major taps on the window, smiles at him, and raises a drink to toast him goodbye.

Robert Pastorelli was asleep on the boardwalk in front of the supply depot. Jack Hangar took his picture while he was sleeping. We were to hang out at the loading dock and wait for direction. Our group was composed of Joe from Minnesota, Tim, Bruce, Harry, Brodie, Jack Kollodge, and Clyde. I had been taking lots of pictures when the cameras were not rolling. At this point my camera battery died.

The film crew decided to do more filming of the Major's suicide. They took a ball bearing and shot it through the window. Then they painted blood, pasted little flecks of something to look like skull bone and dipped a gelatinous substance around the hole to look like brains. Kevin had them tone down the amount of "brains." He said "It looks like a toenail hanging there." They were now ready for our scene where we run over and look in the window. We did this several times although we had to run around the wagon. I was sure the wagon is off camera. No one had seen Dale for some time. "Haven't seen Engelmann for four hours. Presumed lost!" Bruce said. The wind had died down to nothing. It seemed it just kept getting hotter and hotter.

While the film crew was setting up for the next scene, we went with Tim and Dan into the Headquarters building and used their cameras to take their pictures as they posed behind the desks. The room looked authentic and it appeared all the furnishings were antiques.

The next scene was Dunbar and Timmons riding out of the fort on the wagon. Six mules were hooked up. The mules were well behaved.

Kevin and Pastorelli were up on the box; but the real driver was down below them and hidden from view. The reins went through a slit under the box; Pastorelli held fake reins. As they drove off, we did our job of carrying crates and boxes. I carried cartridge boxes from one pile and stacked them on another pile. The fake flour sacks (filled with a fine sawdust) were very dusty and a lot of us were sneezing.

The blacksmith shop was up and running with a blacksmith working at a real forge. He continued hammering even when the crew was not filming. They had tried to herd the longhorn cattle close to the corner of the blacksmith shop; but most of them did not want to cooperate. Something had gone wrong. Kevin came walking back alone and as he passed us, he was muttering to himself.

There were many shots of us loading and unloading. I said we should be singing the Banana Boat Song. I lost count of how many times we did this scene. At one point when we ran up to the window to look in to see what had happened, one of the cavalry soldiers got someone else's saber scabbard between his legs, then down his boot. We were getting punchy and saying a lot of silly things.

"Is this the lunch line?" someone joked.

"I don't want to have to clean up this mess!" I said.

Robert Pastorelli had been sleeping on the boardwalk again. He woke up and was walking away. I ran up to him and asked if I could get my picture taken with him. "Why, it's good old Muttonhead! Of course, I'd like to have my picture taken with you!" He put his arm around my shoulders as Bruce and Tim blazed away with their cameras.

The following is a short real-time sketch of the set at 6:30 p.m.

The film crew is setting up a scene with the buffalo hunters. The sun is low on the western horizon. It is hard to look in that direction. I sit on a cartridge case at the back end of the supply depot loading dock, facing the blacksmith shop. Bruce paces behind me. It is so hot!! The longhorns and horses stand as statues. A slight breeze begins to blow. The buffalo hunters and cavalry soldiers quietly talk, just standing by or sitting on their horses. The people in front of me talk about heading to Rapid City for supper and dancing. Dan walks by and wants to know why I am writing. The filming at Ft Hays is different from the filming of the Civil War battles; but it is just as much fun.

We were done for the day after a short buffalo hunters scene. Kevin rode by in a vehicle and said goodbye to us. I got a ride back to camp in one of the vans.

Andy Cannon held a meeting at the mess tent with all the military and civilian reenactors. The sun had gone down. There were still a few minutes of twilight.

Andy told us we did so well we were ahead of schedule. Unfortunately they were going to have to let some of us go. First, Andy asked for volunteers who did not want to or could not work on Monday. Only three people including Bruce who had to be back at work on Monday raised their hands. This was not enough. Andy was going to have to make some hard decisions. Tim had planned to go home with Bruce; but he found out the film crew needed him for more inside shots. He did not know what to do; but decided to initially plan on staying.

"All dismounted cavalry are cut. Sorry fellas; but I have to do it somehow," Andy said. Well, I was out. I felt disappointed; but had to remember I had been very much involved and had had my mug in front of the camera plenty of times. Mike O'Connel was taking it very hard. Then Andy communicated with the directors on his radio and found he had to reverse his decision. Dismounted cavalry had to stay if they were working on the loading dock in the last scenes. This meant I was back in—all within five minutes! Mike was still out. They kept in all mounted cavalry. Poor Dale was out. Even though he was mounted today in place of Rod, Jack considered Rod mounted and Dale dismounted and since Dale was not in the loading dock scene, he was very much out. All the buffalo hunters who were not in the last scene were out. Hard decisions—I was glad I did not have to make them.

We finished off Allan's hamburger and ate Tim's beef sausage. Allan had been cut from further filming and decided to leave tonight for Waubay Lakes in the northeastern part of the state. He would have a long night drive ahead of him.

Tim and I drove to the convenience store and called our wives. Liz, Helen, and the kids were in Rapid City staying at a Super 8 Motel. I would camp out tonight and drive into town tomorrow morning to be with them. Tim talked to Jan about being in the movie Monday—she told him to go for it. He is going to ride back to Pierre tomorrow with Bruce and Dale, since his grandmother is in town from Arizona and then he will drive back out to the set Sunday night.

Few people were in camp. The night was warm. We sat in Bruce's trailer, talking and joking. We were tired and went to bed early. The moon was so bright—it was almost like daylight.

September 17, 1989, Sunday

A pack of barking dogs out on the set, woke me about 7:00 a.m. The sun was rising in the clear blue sky. A slight breeze blew.

I said goodbye to the Pierre people who would be leaving later in the morning and drove into Rapid City to see Liz, the kids, and my mother in law.

Later that morning, I drove back out to Caputa with the family. I wanted to show them the camp and possibly the set. The gate was unguarded and open. We drove past camp and then past Base Camp. Only prairie dogs stood guard. We got all the way to the set. A guard was there. I stopped the vehicle.

"Is it okay if we look around?" I asked "I've been working here and wanted to show my family the set."

"No one is really supposed to be here," the guard hesitated then said "But if you're quick, you can walk around as long as you don't move anything or go in the buildings."

"Thanks, we'll be careful."

We got out of the van and walked around the set. They liked looking at everything. As we were leaving, we met Dean Semmler, in charge of filming. He was taking photographs of different props. He had filmed *Out Of Africa* and *Lonesome Dove*.

"How do you like the set?" he asked. We told him we really liked it. I said I was a reenactor and told him what I had done in the Civil War scene. He said those shots had turned out well.

We returned to Rapid City. Liz and Helen went shopping at the Rushmore Mall. I took the kids to Reptile Gardens. They liked petting the snakes and ponies, looking at the alligators and crocodiles, and riding the tortoises. We returned to the mall and met Liz and Helen. After more shopping and eating, they returned to Pierre. I felt sad and lonely seeing them go.

Jack Hangar had invited me to his motel room. Jack, Clyde, Dan, and Dave were watching football. No one was interested in taking a ride up into the Black Hills. They had been out on the town late last night.

I took off by myself and drove up into the Hills on Mt. Rushmore Road and took a left on Twin Springs Road. I had never been back this road before and it was fun exploring new territory. I reached a T in the road and took a left toward Keystone. The road followed a creek and old railroad track. It was a nice wooded drive with an occasional old shack.

To my right appeared a sight that made me hit the brakes and back up. There was a huge wood carving over ten feet tall of a bear with three cubs. The bear was standing erect and the cubs were hanging on it.

The road continued to wind along the creek until it ended in the tourist town of Keystone. I took a left on 16A and headed back toward the four lane highway. I could not believe my eyes. The Department of Transportation was straightening and widening the road–hillsides were blasted away, trees were bulldozed over into large piles. It looked terrible. This was being done to make it an easier drive up to Mt. Rushmore.

I arrived back at camp at dusk. Clouds had rolled in so it was darker than usual. The wind had blown down my tent. I had to put it back up in the dark. Dave, Dan, and I scraped together odds and ends for supper and ate in the dark. The clouds broke and we could see better with the full moon's light.

R.L. Curtin had come by to look at the picture of his mules and hospital wagon that I had taken at the hospital set. I told him I would send him a copy. R.L. was a former marine who ran a cavalry school in Montana. He talked about what they did at school and how it was good we were involved in this movie. He said if we stick with it, we will probably have a lot more movie job offers.

I found John Arrasmith from Kentucky who has made arrows for the movie. He made both Sioux and Pawnee arrows the way the Indians used to. He said he would make two of each kind of arrow for me. John said Indians come to him to find out how arrows were made in the old way. He showed me other things he had made including fake human trigger fingers. The Indians would cut off the trigger finger of someone they killed in battle and would make a necklace out of them. We talked about the Old West. He was very knowledgeable about Native American religion.

Dave, Dan, and I went to the buckskinner's campfire. It was another night of singing songs and telling jokes.

The full moon shone bright. The fire crackled. Sparks flew in a slight breeze.

Tim Teegerstrom told a good joke.

"A city slicker was speeding along in his car in the country. He was looking for a certain fellow to collect a delinquent payment. He stopped to ask a farmer who was plowing a field with a mule where this person lived. The farmer wouldn't tell him. The city slicker pulled out a pistol and said 'I'd like to see you dance.' and shot six shots into the dirt around the farmer's feet making him dance. When the city slicker's gun was out of bullets, the farmer reached around the other side of the mule, pulled out a shotgun, leveled it at the city slicker, and said 'Ever kiss a mule on the lips?' 'No.' answered the city slicker 'But it's something I've always wanted to try.'"

The crowd roared with laughter.

There was a wide variety of songs. One was about two women coming upon a sleeping Scotsman wearing a kilt. Another was the old sea chantey, "Nelson's Blood", with the chorus of "And we'll row the old chariots along, we'll row the old chariots along, we'll row the old chariots along, and we'll all hang on behind."

Another song—Blue Hawk sang a line then we responded with "Haul em away."

"Little Sally Racket."

"Haul em away."

"Sailed aboard a packet."

"Haul em away."

"And she never did regret it."

"Haul em away."

"And oh dee high ho!"

"Haul em away."

"And oh dee high ho!"

"Haul em away."

We went through about five verses of this.

"Those are sea chanteys from the 1700's," Blue Hawk said. "Some of them songs could have made it to the rendezvous too. Cause a lot of guys jumped ship in those days."

"Yeah, look at Hugh Glass. He came up from the south," Tim said.

More jokes were told—plenty of laughter around the fire. More songs of fur trapping and discussions of the hardships of trapping beaver in cold streams.

"Are you ready for Hungry Child?" Blue Hawk asked. "This is death and destruction."

The crowd was ready.

"This was sung by people coming out of England in ships to get away from their problems. This would be about the 1700's—the old days."

"Back before the hula hoop!" Tim said.

"Yeah."

"Willow hula hoops!" Rabi said.

Blue Hawk and Belinda started the song and the group grew quiet with the haunting words.

"… The young child started crying 'Mother I'm hungry. Mother dear give me bread or I'll be dying.'

'Wait my child. Wait my child for tomorrow we'll be plowing.'"

The verses ran from plowing to planting, planting to reaping, reaping to grinding, grinding to baking, and ending with

"… and when the bread was warm in the oven, the child lay cold in his coffin."

The only sound was the crackling fire. Some people began to stand up to leave.

"Well if everybody's breaking up, then we have to send this off right!" said Blue Hawk.

"What's it now?" asked Belinda.

"Since we're ending the evening."

"Happy trails to you until we meet again," Tim sang.

"Twas the night before Christmas and all through the house," Blue Hawk began,

"The whole cotton pickin' family was drunk as a louse …"

The poetic parody went downhill from there; but sent everyone back to their tents and teepees chuckling and laughing.

Tim Larson returned about 10:30 p.m. It seemed as if he had not been gone at all. The night was warmer than the previous nights. Tim stayed in my tent and we were in our bags by 11:30 p.m.

September 18, 1989, Monday

We were awaken at 5:00 a.m. by the worst bugling I have ever heard in my life. I think I could have done a better job and I do not even know how to play a bugle.

We got dressed and ate a breakfast of scrambled eggs, sausage, biscuits and gravy, and plenty of coffee. Dogs circled the tables hoping for a scrap of food to fall or be thrown their way. One dog came around every morning wearing a different bandanna around his neck. I guess he was making a fashion statement.

We talked and joked with the buckskinners until the bus came to take us out to Base Camp. I found Kathy Smith who was with wardrobe and asked if her *Dances With Wolves* pendants were in. She said yes; but not to tell any of the production crew since she had a limited amount made at that point and wanted to give them to the extras first. So I bought two, one for Liz and one for Mom.

I asked Dave Silva to sign my *Dances With Wolves* book.

"Why do you want my autograph? I'm not famous!" he said.

"Well, I wanted people's autographs in the book who I've worked with on the set. And I'm sure you're going to be big one of these days," I answered.

After a short wait, the bus took us to the set. We had a lot of time to kill. All the scenes were inside the Headquarters building so we were not needed the whole morning.

Jim Hatzell had been sketching people's portraits. He was working on the portrait of a Native American with long braided hair. He told us his name was Jimmy Herman and he played the part of Stone Calf. Jimmy joked about not making it all the way through the movie since his character is killed in a battle with the Pawnees. Later Jim sketched a portrait of me. Everyone said it was a good likeness. Jim sketched Tim as he looked for the inside desk job shot.

The day started out cool; but soon became hot. I sat at the tables and talked with the soldiers and then crossed the parade ground and talked with the buckskinners who were sitting in the shade of the bath house. They told stories of trapping, skinning, and rendezvous. They told me the basics of what I would need to get into a modern day rendezvous—my shirt was okay, a pair of linen pants and that would be about it. I could add on from there. They thought it was great I associated with them. They said most people who were not buckskinners were apprehensive to talk to them. "They must think we are mean and dangerous." Finally it was lunch. We were fed roast beef. It was great.

The following is an afternoon real-time sketch of the set while we waited for filming to begin.

A few of the buckskinners sit on the side steps of the Headquarters building. One of them holds a book on Indian sign language. They are trying to learn it. Earlier, I had Rabi point his muzzleloader at me while I held up my hands for a picture. One of the buckskinners puts his hat on his horse's head. There is a constant search for shade. I find some on the front porch of the supply depot and pull up an empty chair. Horses whinny to each other. The fragrance of horse manure wafts on the breath of a breeze. Tim Larson is to my left, asleep on a bench. Andy, a kid from Ohio, and Dan discuss the attributes of different cameras. To my left beyond Tim, several people lounge on sacks talking in low tones. Tim is now snoring. Flies buzz around. Two little girls in nineteenth century costume ride by, giggling at something one of them said. A woman in costume lies on the porch trying to sleep while holding onto the reins of two horses. Some set crew members work at various jobs while others stand and talk. Kevin's mother stands on

Quick Sketch
Bauxite, Tuesday
September 14, 1989 South Dakota

HATZELL
1989

the Headquarters porch with some other people. Kevin's double walks out of the building and joins them.

The flags snap as the breeze picks up. Other sounds—someone pours water out of a bucket, boots and spurs on wood planks, and Tim's snores.

John Arrasmith wearing small oval Civil War era sunglasses rides by on his horse. Linda talks to Dave Silva on a walkie-talkie. A sergeant canters by on his horse followed by seven mounted troopers including Skip Harrington.

"Same old story—hurry up and wait!" Skip yells to us.

The film crew was ready to use us by mid-afternoon. They filmed the loading dock scene where we hear the gunshot and run to the Major's window. As we were running the second time, Linda shouted "Freeze!" and had us mark our spots where we froze. This was our number one position that we returned to each time there was a new shot. Those of us who had stopped before reaching the shade, baked in the sun.

The crew now filmed from inside the Major's office as we ran up to the window. The set crew had painted blood running down from the bullet hole in the window, then pasted flecks of fake skull and brain matter around the hole. They used a spray bottle filled with fake blood to create a continuous bloody drip from the bullet hole in the window onto the window sill.

Kevin directed the filming from inside the Major's office. I reached the window and looked in at what was supposed to be the major's dead body. Kids were looking in the window. Old Harry pulled them away. We milled around and speculated on what happened. We did this three times.

"You need to be more animated!" the assistant director said. "Fight for position at the window. Try not to give up your spots. Jostle each other to see what's going on inside."

A barrel was set up for the kids to stand on. This next filming sequence we fought for position at the window as the cameras rolled.

After Harry pulled the kids away, the barrel was kicked over and rolled in my direction. I stood on the side of it and held my position at the window. The inside camera was right on our faces. The film crew liked this shot. "All they had to do was to tell us to act like animals!" I said to Jack.

The film crew was now going to take still photographs of the mounted troops with Kevin for promotional material. The riders formed up on the parade ground by the flag pole. Andy Cannon saw the dismounted troops and told us to get our gear and join them. Kevin was not there yet so I ran back to the supply depot, where I had stowed my gear. I quickly put on the sack coat and waist belt, rushed out onto the boardwalk, and almost ran over a man sitting on the steps. I glanced over my shoulder as I ran out onto the parade ground. The man I had almost run over was Kevin Costner! The dismounted troops stood by the flag pole. Kevin rode out to us and we posed for still pictures.

Tim and Dan told me about the inside scene after the Major shoots himself. They run into the Major's office and stare at the Major's body until an officer pushes them out of the room. "We thought it would be funny if we turned to each other and said 'Oh Boy!'" joked Dan.

After another wait, the sound crew wanted to record sounds and voices from the crowd. They recorded the buffalo hunters' voices at their camp, and slowly walked past the bathhouse and trading post recording additional peoples' voices. These were the sounds Dunbar would hear as he rides into the fort.

Tim and I were at the bathhouse. We argue with the bathhouse women over the price of baths and shaves.

This is crazy! I thought. *I'm pictured twice on the other side of the parade ground—watering horses and eating stew. Now my voice is across the parade ground arguing over the price of a bath!*

Next the crew recorded the sounds of the cavalry riding past. We quietly waited while "Major Lee Depressed" went berserk and screamed inside the Headquarters building. It was getting dusk and clouds had rolled in. I quietly talked with the mounted troopers. "The next scene will be the winter attack on the Sioux village," Jack said. People would need greatcoats and Jack was willing to make them. He said if I was interested in being in the next scene, I should talk to Andy Cannon. The crew finished filming the inside shots and we were done.

On the bus ride back to camp, I sat behind Andy. I asked if he could use me in the next filming sequence. He said yes, all I would need was my uniform and the greatcoat. The production company would provide a horse for me. What great news! It will be filmed in Spearfish Canyon, South Dakota, late October or early November. The whole movie will now be made in South Dakota. Originally the winter scenes were going to be filmed in Montana or Wyoming.

It was dark when we arrived in camp. A light drizzle fell from the sky. I stood in line to receive my pay and then signed up with Marty Cannon, Andy's wife, for "The Search For Dunbar". Jim Hatzell, John Arrasmith, and Blue Hawk waited in line behind me and I said my good-byes to them. Funny how you can form friendships so quickly when thrown into a situation like this.

The rain now came down harder. Tim and I took down the tent and packed our vehicles. We helped Clyde hitch up his horse trailer and said goodbye to Jack and him. They were driving back to Omaha yet tonight. We said goodbye to Paul Williams, Dan, and Dave Bowman.

Lightning flashed across the sky. Tim noticed one of my headlights was out, so I would follow him back to Pierre. We drove down to the teepees and said goodbye to the buckskinners—Elder with his skunk cap, Terry, Tim, and Rich. "Keep your topknot!" was their parting word of advice.

We drove down the road to Caputa. Even with the heavy rain, there was still a lot of dust. We stopped at Wall and bought coffee and candy bars.

I was very tired and had the window down and the radio blaring on a rock and roll station. It was still hard to stay awake and concentrate. A highway patrol officer stopped me for the missing headlight and gave me a warning and ten days notice to get it fixed. The rain became intense. To make matters worse, my windshield wipers were not wiping off the water, but smearing it. I was glad I had Tim's taillights to follow. Several times we saw deer in the ditch.

After what seemed an eternity, the lights of Pierre appeared in the distance. As I entered the city limits, the city police stopped me for the headlight. The police were doing their job. I arrived home at 1:30 a.m., woke Liz, and gave her the *Dances With Wolves* pendant as an early wedding anniversary present. I related filming highlights to her as I drifted off to sleep.

CHAPTER 6 BETWEEN TIMES

◆

September 19, 1989, Tuesday-October 31, 1989, Tuesday

Everyday work was a depressing drudgery compared to movie-making. Dale, Bruce, and Tim decided not to apply for "The Search for Dunbar." Andy Cannon told me there would not be any production horses for my use. If I wanted to be in the scene, I would have to find my own horse and gear.

Clyde Kocher from Nebraska was returning for the filming. I contacted him and he was willing to rent me one of his horses. Since Jack Hangar was not going to return for this scene, he rented me his McCllean saddle, saddle blanket, and tack which Skip Harrington and Joe Acamo would bring along. As soon as I had the horse and gear confirmed, I let Andy know and I was in the scene.

"The Search for Dunbar" was to take place during the winter. Jack Hanger was making me a sack coat and greatcoat. The greatcoat was a heavy wool coat soldiers wore during the winter months. Jack would send the coats with Skip and Joe.

I ordered a black, felt, broad-brimmed Hardee hat from Jarningans. When the hat arrived, I opened the box and pulled it out. It looked like something a pilgrim would have worn. I steamed it and slouched down the brim in the front and back and formed the crown.

November 1, 1989, Wednesday

Andy Cannon called to confirm I was on for the movie. He said to be at the Super 8 Motel outside the town of Spearfish, South Dakota at noon next Tuesday.

CHAPTER 7 THE SEARCH FOR DUNBAR

◆

November 7, 1989, Tuesday

I got up at 7:00 a.m. and packed my gear into our GMC Jimmy.

"Now I want you to be good," I told three year old Chris. "I want you to be the man of the house while I'm gone and take care of Mommy and Becky. Okay?"

"Uh huh," he answered.

As I was heading out the door I asked "Chris, do you remember what I told you?"

"Yes! I am king of the house!"

I said goodbye to Liz and the kids and left Pierre about 8:30 a.m. The one-hundred-and-sixty mile trip on Highway 34 across the prairie to the town of Sturgis was uneventful. One small herd of antelope stood on a distant ridge. Traffic was almost nonexistent. The Black Hills with Bear Butte in the foreground appeared and gradually grew larger at my approach. This is my favorite road to the Hills.

I stopped in Sturgis for gas and some Sturgis jerky. It is the best commercial jerky I have ever eaten. Sturgis is famous for its annual motorcycle rally.

I drove to the Super 8 Motel outside of Spearfish where we were to meet for the movie. I checked at the desk and was directed to Andy Cannon's room at the pool level.

Andy sat behind a card table. A line of reenactors stood in front of the table waiting for their turn to sign in. I joined the line behind Buck Buxton and Paul Williams.

Andy explained the filming would take place up in the Black Hills in Spearfish Canyon. Highway 222 had been closed from Savoy to the intersection of 134. A Lakota village was set up on the road between Roughlock Falls and the Rod and Gun Campground. The horse corrals were set up to the south on the road between Rod and Gun Campground and Timon Campground. Horse trailers would have to be brought in from the back end. In other words they would have to take a long circular route and come up behind the canyon, because the production company did not want traffic through the village. In the morning we would meet at the lobby and be bussed to Savoy at 5:30 a.m. At Savoy, breakfast would be served at 6:00 a.m., we would have a half hour to eat. After breakfast we would be bussed to the north side of the Lakota village. We would then walk through the village up to the horse corrals, catch our horses and saddle up. The production company will pay for our rooms at the Super 8.

It was my turn to sign in.

"Hi Bill," Andy said. "Bill Stevens and I were just talking about you."

"Yeah, Bill's a nice guy. How's he doing?"

"Good. We need to share rooms to cut down on cost. Is there anyone that you are rooming with?"

"No."

"Let's see," Andy said as he looked at his list. "How about if I put you in with John Arrasmith?"

"Great!" John was playing a scout.

"Okay, I've asked that everyone show up by the pool this evening dressed in their gear, so I can look them over."

Paul had to take his horse, Shiloh, up to the corrals. Since I did not have anything to do, I offered to ride along. He was happy to have company since he did not know the back roads that well. Andy gave us a map to the corrals. He was told the roads had been icy and hard to travel yesterday. No one was sure what condition they were in now.

We drove through the town of Spearfish and took a left on Hills View Road. There was no snow in the foothills; but we could see snow higher up. We turned left on Forest Service Road 134 and gradually climbed upward as we headed South. It became cooler, large patches of snow appeared and soon the whole ground was covered. The road had become icy.

We caught up to other slower moving pickup trucks pulling horse trailers also heading to the movie set corrals. The caravan of vehicles was climbing a steep incline, the lead pickup and trailer lost momentum and came to a halt on the ice. All the other vehicles were too close and had to hit the brakes. One pickup and trailer slid into the ditch. Paul was far enough behind that we did not become trapped with the others. With the aid of his four-wheel drive, Paul weaved in and out of the stopped vehicles until we reached higher ground with good gravel where we came to a stop.

We walked back to the mess on the hill to offer help. Paul asked if anyone had a tow chain. There was one. One pickup was unhooked from its trailer to help start pulling the others. We helped push the one out of the ditch. They had plenty of help on the other vehicles so we continued on our way.

A mile farther up the road, we came upon another stranded vehicle and horse trailer. Two men were leading a horse away from the trailer. We slowed down as we passed to see if they needed help; but they waved us on. The road conditions continued to deteriorate. The snow and ice were greater. The sky was becoming more cloudy.

We talked about McClellan saddles, horses, *Dances With Wolves* of course, and the upcoming movie *Son of the Morning Star* which was about the battle of the Little Big Horn. We passed Highway 222 to Iron Creek Lake and knew we were over half way to our destination. After a few harrowing slips and slides, we reached 222 through the canyon and

turned left down Spearfish Canyon. We passed Timon Campground on the right and soon arrived at the horse corrals. They were set up on the road. One other group was unloading their horses.

Bob Erickson was in charge at the corrals. He was from Montana and had helped Andy Cannon on the other movie sets. Bob had a camper set up and was spending the nights there to watch the horses.

Bob told us that the U.S. Forest Service said the corrals had to be set up on the road and no where else, so we were restricted for space. Paul had brought along his own panels to set up a corral for Shiloh. Bob showed us where we could set up the corral which was in front of the larger corrals that held the production horses. After we had it set up we carried over two hay bales for Shiloh. A pump brought water from Little Spearfish Creek to water the horses out of large watering troughs.

Bob asked if we could help him set up some more corrals. We walked to the opposite end of the corrals to a stack of panels. As we began setting up a new corral, dark clouds rolled in and started an intense snow shower that lasted for a half hour.

Those who had been stuck on the road were starting to arrive. On our way back to Spearfish, we passed Clyde Kocher and his son Steve who were bringing up our horses.

The clouds broke up and it became warmer as we descended out of the Hills to town. It was still considerably cooler than this morning and the wind blew stronger.

As we pulled into the Super 8 Motel parking lot, Skip Harrington and Joe Acamo were unloading Skip's car. They had the saddle and tack I was renting from Jack Hangar and my sack coat and greatcoat Jack had made along with a lot of greatcoats he had made for other people. I helped them carry their clothes and equipment up to their room. They brought me a saddle, bridle, two blankets, and a sling for the carbine that I would get from props.

There were problems with Jack's greatcoats. The first problem was a lack of buttons. Each greatcoat was to have twelve brass eagle buttons down the front and smaller brass eagle buttons on the cape's edge. Jack had ordered buttons from Pakistan; but they did not arrive in time for filming. Fortunately for me, Jack had pinned six buttons inside a sleeve of my greatcoat. He had also put four buttons in the pocket of my sack coat. Buttons were worth their weight in gold and I had ten of them for two coats.

The next problem was Jack did not have enough cloth to make capes for all the coats. A bolt of cloth Jack had received had large holes cut in the fabric in the middle of the bolt. Joe and Skip brought samples along to show people. Jack's pattern for the coats was off and there was about six inches too much in the front. Skip and Joe had stopped at Jim Hatzell's house in Rapid City where they had tried to make alterations to some of the greatcoats. Jack said he would alter the greatcoats for those who want them altered and would make capes for those that were missing. He would send all buttons to the greatcoat buyers when they arrived. Poor Skip and Joe had to listen to a lot of complaining from angry greatcoat buyers.

R.L. Curtin from Montana came into Skip and Joe's room to get his greatcoat. He thanked me for pictures of his mules and hospital wagon I had sent him. He was concerned about the inside burlap liner of his greatcoat. Skip answered that burlap was what the army contractors used to make the inside liners.

I took the saddle, blankets, and bridle to my room which was a few doors down from Skip and Joe. John Arrasmith was there. He helped me bring in my gear. John was dressed in buckskin clothing. During the whole time we were together, I never saw him dressed in modern day clothes. He said he was late with my arrows, because he knew I would prefer arrows actually used in the movie. "Of course!" I answered. John said it would take some time to get those.

"How old do you think my buckskin shirt is?" he asked.

"Well, anywhere from a hundred years to yesterday. I have no idea," I answered.

"I made it last week!"

"Wow! It looks pretty old!"

He had brain-tanned the shirt. Its smoky fragrance filled the room.

I went down to the motel's lower level to Fred Newcomb's room. Fred was from Orange, California, and had brought along leather gear and weapons for me—a saber, scabbard, belt, cap pouch, colt revolver, and holster. He showed me how to strap it all on. I went back to my room to get ready for pool-side inspection.

John's clothing was interesting. Besides the buckskin shirt, he wore a musk ox cape that came from above the Arctic Circle. It had been traded through several tribes until he bought it from the Blackfeet of Montana. On his head he wore a broad-brimmed hat, turned up in the front with a red feather attached to it that signified scout. He wore leather pants and buffalo hide boots with the woolly hair on the outside. He tucked two ivory handled pistols in his belt and slung a cartridge bandoleer over his shoulder across his chest. He carried a Henry rifle.

My clothes consisted of the following (although I did not wear the unseen portions during inspection so I would not roast). First long underwear, a pair of cotton socks and a pair of wool socks, a print shirt from the period (three buttons in front), wool pants, suspenders, wool sack coat, wool greatcoat, Hardee hat, saber belt and everything that goes with it that I described earlier, and the carbine sling. My gloves were not authentic—they were leather—to be authentic I should have had gauntlets. I did not have cavalry boots; but did have my brogan shoes that were worn by the cavalry during the Civil War. Strapped to my shoes were old cavalry spurs that Helen, my mother-in-law, had given me. I was worried the old worn leather would not last; but it did.

We gathered at pool-side and waited as Andy looked us over. The majority of clothes and gear looked good. Andy told certain people to "lose" items that did not fit the Civil War era.

Walt from Montana had a new black cowboy hat with the brim turned up on the sides. Andy told him to turn down the brim and slouch down the front; but Walt refused saying it was a new hat.

Andy gave us the details for tomorrow morning that I have already described. They would give a general 4:30 a.m. wake-up call.

"I hope it won't be by a bugler!" someone said in a loud voice.

We needed to be on the bus by 5:30 a.m. Those of us who had saddles and tack at the motel needed to get those items up to the corrals separate from the bus. Someone volunteered to take them up the back way earlier in the morning. Andy would pay gas and mileage. We were to load up the gear tonight.

Andy dismissed the group. I went back to my room and stripped off the hot, heavy wool coats. Skip had given me a gray blanket that I rolled up in my black poncho and strapped to the pommel of the saddle. I strapped my tin cup to the back of the saddle. We were to appear as if we had been out in the field for a long time. Joe, Skip, and I took our gear outside and found the pickup that would carry our saddles and tack up to the set.

An icy wind blew. It would be cold tomorrow morning up in the Hills.

We walked up to The Sluice Restaurant to eat. The Sluice was designed to resemble an old mine and contained artifacts from the nineteenth century gold mining era. I had recommended it to John and a few others. We entered wearing our uniforms and hats. The place was full of reenactors wearing their uniforms. Reenactors outnumbered people wearing modern clothing. Frank Costanza from Montana had shaved off his beard and mustache for this scene. Frank said he felt naked.

Joe, Skip, and I sat together at a table. Joe was wearing a blue and white stripped shirt with canvas collar and cuffs he had made. We discussed everything from the upcoming movie *Son of the Morning Star* to religion.

They were interested in my Schwenkfelder Church background. Casper Schwenkfeld was a church reformer contemporary with Martin Luther. Over the years the ruling authorities persecuted Schwenkfeld's followers. In 1734 the Schwenkfelders fled their native Silesia to William Penn's colony where they were guaranteed religious freedom. I am one of their descendants.

Private
Sherman

Gordon
AVE ACEDO

Enlisted to Private, Ninth Shenandoah
in the national convention? Also #3
"Souther colors" August 27th 1969

Quick
Second

Self construction

(practise of 2nd regiment, 2 military of 3rd column)
Southern "Southern marchings" August 26, 1969
at the day of the film "Darkest with armies"

One of Skip's grandfathers was a Native American. Skip also had an ancestor who was in the cavalry and was killed at the Little Big Horn—a Lieutenant Harrington. He believed he had ancestors on both sides of the fight at the Little Big Horn.

The food was good but it took forever to get our bills and then to get change.

Skip was waiting in line to pay and was standing behind R.L.

"R.L., I understand you're the Donkey Man."

"No one calls me a Donkey Man," he stepped closer to Skip. "Are you calling me a Donkey Man?"

"I'm not calling you a Donkey Man," Skip held up his hands, backing away. "I'm only repeating what Pastorelli said on the Carson Show."

Robert Pastorelli had explained on the Johnny Carson Show that he had called R.L. a Donkey Man and R.L. had corrected him telling him he was a mule driver. R.L. continued to press Skip.

"Look if you're just joking around fine; but if this is for real, I again apologize and don't want to fight you," Skip said. R.L. backed off.

When I got back to the room, John asked if I minded having a 4:15 a.m. wake-up call since it would take him a long time to get ready. "No problem," I said. I would just as soon be early than late. John was going to go to bed right away; it was about 9:30 p.m.

I had buttons to sew. I did not want to disturb John, so I took my coats down the hall to Skip and Joe's room. They were staying up for a while and coached me on sewing the buttons and button holes. I started with the greatcoat. The first button I positioned wrong and got it on the cape and not below the collar. Skip marked on the coats where to sew the buttons. I was able to sew them on at the right spots; but I did not always get the eagles facing the right way. The button holes on the coat were already stitched in and all I had to do was open them with a knife.

A constant stream of people visited Skip and Joe including Paul Williams, Jim Hatzell, and R.L. They talked on all manner of subjects.

HATZELL
1980

Quick
Sketch

Remembered Tuesday Evening
November 7, 1980
Rapid City, S. Dakota

I began to work on the sack coat buttons and button holes. Joe showed me the right way to sew fabric around the hole. I was tired and did a sloppy job.

Skip brought out his haversack and dumped a pile of necklaces onto the bed. They were all Native American and for the most part old. To me the most interesting was a necklace made of Italian glass beads Skip said had been traded by Lewis and Clark. He said he had it documented that these beads were only traded on the Lewis and Clark expedition. A collector had offered him $50 a bead. There were a lot of beads on the string. On another necklace was a peace medallion from the 1750's with the image of King George II on one side. On the other side an Indian and white man sat on the ground facing each other. The white man wore a broad-brimmed Quaker hat. Skip had acquired most of the necklaces from a Canadian museum that had closed. What neat things! But I could not pay close attention—I had to sew.

I had three buttons and three button holes completed. Skip fell asleep as he was talking. My eyes were going out of focus. I could not see to sew the last button and hole.

It was midnight when I got back to the room. I was quiet and did not wake John.

November 8, 1989, Wednesday

4:15 a.m., the wake-up call came too soon. I was bone tired. We got dressed in the manner I have already described.

I picked up two coffees in the lobby and took them back to the room. We were ready long before it was time to go, so we sipped our coffees and talked. The wool uniform and greatcoat were hot.

5:30 a.m. rolled around and amazingly enough, everyone was ready to go. An old school bus was waiting outside for us. No one was to drive their own vehicles unless they had permission. Dave Silva directed us onto the bus. It was very cold outside. I was tired and dozed during the ride up through Spearfish Canyon. John did not think I would make it through the day: "You look real bad."

We reached Savoy where the road up towards Roughlock Falls was closed to through traffic because of the movie. The old Latch String Inn had been torn down by Homestake Mining Company—it was a shame but it had become structurally unsound and could not be saved. The bus pulled into the South Dakota Department of Transportation gravel parking lot. We were told to get off the bus. It was hard getting on and off the bus since we wore heavy wool uniforms and had all kinds of guns and swords that we had to deal with not to mention spurs on our boots.

The catering mobile was there with its familiar generator humming to provide the energy to cook our morning repast. We stood in line as the darkness turned to a gray morning light. The caterers handed each of us in turn a Styrofoam container from out of the high window. Someone opened theirs to see what it was. We would have been disappointed if it had not been scrambled eggs, bacon, biscuits and gravy. Don't get me wrong—I really liked it. We could also have fruit and cereal. I picked up orange juice and coffee. Some of the others grumbled but still ate. I came to the conclusion that you can provide people with a fun exciting situation, feed them good, and even pay them, and they will still find something to grumble about.

We ate in a large tent at long tables and quickly devoured our food. It felt colder inside the tent than outside.

After eating I grabbed a second steaming cup of coffee and waited outside until we were told to get back on the school bus. As the bus driver drove us past Roughlock Falls, we could smell a stinking, burning smell—he had forgotten to release the emergency brake.

The bus stopped on the south side of the falls. We got out and began walking up the road past the various trucks—props, wardrobe, makeup, and other vehicles I had no idea what their purpose was. We walked past the Native American bus. They looked like they still had to get ready.

We rounded a bend in the road and there was the Lakota village. What a sight. There were probably twenty teepees. They looked realistic and well used. Some were set up on the road. Trees had been brought in to stand on the road to disguise it from the cameras. Most of the teepees were on the far side of Little Spearfish Creek. We had passed a dump truck full of snow that I assumed they used to cover up modern cables and equipment. We walked past Rod and Gun Campground and soon came to the corral area. Clyde's horses were by the line shack in a small corral Paul and I had put together. There was an awful lot of snow.

"Well Bill, I think I'll have you ride Bud," said Clyde. He pointed out a bay with a scar on his forehead and handed me a halter. I caught the horse and led him out of the pen. I rubbed Bud on the neck and behind the ears and quietly talked to him.

"Are we going to be friends?" His ears changed from back to forwards. "Yeah, we'll be buds." I was a little concerned about how I would do since it had been a few years since I last rode. I used to ride all the time when I was a kid. I led Bud, following Skip and his horse, Starlight, to the watering trough. Bud was excited, probably because of all the other horses and a strange human. I saddled Bud and asked Skip to make sure I had him saddled properly.

"Just thought I'd let you know ol' Bud's dumped the last three people who tried to ride him," Skip said as he checked the cinch. This was a confidence builder. Clyde put the bridle on Bud because Bud did not like to take a bit. Clyde was the only person who could get him to do it.

Skip, Joe, and I were the first ones to be ready. Andy Cannon told us to form up at the Rod and Gun Campground. The three of us lead our horses down there. I did not want to rush Bud. When we got there, Skip and Joe mounted up. I started to swing into the saddle. I had no sooner swung my right leg over Bud's right side, and my foot had not yet reached the stirrup, when Bud started to buck. I held on to my seat and was able to ride it out. After that, Bud never tried to buck me off again. I felt good knowing I had stayed on his back. I walked him around for exercise and had him do some trotting. Other riders started to arrive.

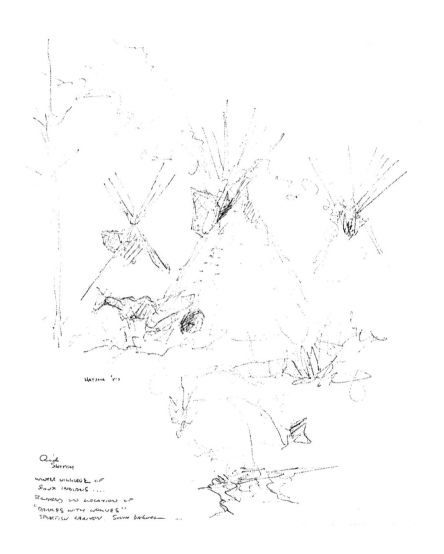

HATSON '93

Quick
Sketch

WINTER VILLAGE OF
SIOUX INDIANS . . . .
RENDERED ON LOCATION OF
"DANCES WITH WOLVES"
SPEARFISH CANYON, SOUTH DAKOTA . . .

Mike Terry, who was portraying a scout with John, was riding his production horse down the road. The horse acted up, started to buck, and threw him. The horse would not settle down, so Mike went back and got another horse. Bud was afraid of John's musk ox cape; but became used to it as the day went on.

It was hard taking pictures from on top of the horse. First I had to take the glove off my right hand then reach through the front of the greatcoat and pull the camera out of the sack coat pocket. There were only so many angles you could turn in the saddle to take the picture. Getting the camera back in the pocket was a problem also. I finally stopped trying to put it in the sack coat pocket and let it ride in my greatcoat above the saber belt.

They had us form up into three companies. I was in the first company. They had us line up and count off by fours. We formed up on a rider carrying the guidon, a small flag on a staff, to my left and the First Sergeant to my right. The horses' heads were to be in a straight line and we were to be stirrup to stirrup. The horses jostled each other. Knees crunched other knees; but amazingly it worked out well. They had us perform some drills through the campground. I had no idea what we were doing; but followed along. We formed up on the road again and were allowed to rest. I checked the cinch on Bud and tightened it. I noticed R.L. was scrambling up the loose rock slope under the cliffs.

"R.L. do you see a trail?" Andy shouted.

"I think we can make it up here." he answered. R.L. was about a fourth of the way up the slope. I had climbed that slope twice in the past and was sure there was no way a horse could make it to the top in that area. There was a trailhead at the campground cul de sac; but it wound around and would take some time to get to the top. I told Andy this and they stopped trying to go straight up the side of the canyon. They would try the long route later.

A pickup truck arrived with carbines. Those of us who did not have carbines fell out and rode over to the truck. Andy handed them to us.

The carbine had a ring on the stock. The ring hooks to a snap on the carbine sling that crosses from the left shoulder to the right hip. The carbine hangs down the right side of the horse. Almost everyone had small leather rings called sockets that the carbine barrel slipped into so it would not slap against the horse's flank. My saddle did not have one, so I held it steady with my right hand as I rode.

Andy had the two scouts and the first ten men of our company fall out to leave for a shot. The last of the ten was Skip who was on my immediate right and who had been helping me. They left up the trail-head. Keith, a big lieutenant, was left in charge and continued to drill us. "Right face!" he ordered which meant I was in the lead. I knew absolutely nothing! I told this to Keith. "Keep your position," he said. At times he would ride alongside me; but at other times I was by myself. We walked and trotted. Most of the time it was a fast trot. Bud liked to trot; but when walking, he was very slow. There was no such command as "Forward Ho!" That did not come about until World War I. The commands were "Forward march!" "To the right march!" "To the left march!" I was starting to get the hang of it. I just hoped there were not too many other more difficult maneuvers we would need to learn.

The others came back to join us and we stopped our practice. We formed up in a line and were given the "At ease!" command. The crew had filmed the others in a saber charge through the trees and snow.

Something in the snow spooked John's horse. The horse jumped straight up and tore off down the slope through the evergreen trees. John went flying off the horse hanging on to his Henry. He hit the ground hard on his side; but was okay. The horse went flying down the hill, and scraped a tree ripping off the saddle. Eyewitnesses said it looked like the saddle exploded. Someone gave John an Indian name, Takes His Saddle With Him. The horse had run back toward us. Several riders caught the horse and calmed it down. The film crew had captured the whole incident on film.

After loosening the cinch and moving the saddle blanket and saddle forward on Bud, I tightened the cinch again and climbed back in the saddle. I heard a loud "Thwamp!" to my left. Joe lay on his back in the snow. Unknown to him, his saddle's cinch had worked loose and as he was getting up in the saddle, it slid to the side and threw him to the ground.

There was a long wait. Both Bud and I dozed. I was not cold, not even my feet. The film crew was finally ready for us, so we rode up to the trailhead and headed south parallel to the road. We rode single file on the trail. The crew did not want us to get off the trail into the fresh snow. The file of horses and riders entered a small clearing and passed a camera. We kept on walking until we were about a hundred yards from the camera, then turned to face the way we had come, and formed up into columns of two.

In this scene, we ride through the deep snow at a fast trot. The troopers in front have their sabers drawn. The rest of us have our carbines on our hips, barrels pointing straight up—at the ready. We are to keep the horses head to tail. The riders paired together are to keep stirrup to stirrup.

"Have intense determined looks on your faces. For months you have been chasing the Indians and have finally caught them," the assistant director said.

On the first take Joe's cinch was loose again and he came uncorked off his horse. He sat out the rest of this scene's filming.

We did this scene over several times. When each shot was done, the Captain ordered "Halt!" We would retrace our steps back to the start and film it again.

The sun was bright, the snow deep, the colors intense—the scene should look great. During another scene, the film crew had us split the column in two when we came to a large rock, each side riding single file on either side of the rock. When we were done, we rode in one column back to the campground. We formed up in line and were put at ease.

HATZELL...
SOUTH DAKOTA

I started to get off Bud to check the cinch. I forgot the Sharps carbine dangling down the right side of Bud, still attached to me. I had my right foot on the ground, left foot still in the stirrup, and the carbine on the far side of Bud. I was strapped flush against his left side. Bud did not like this arrangement. He started to swivel and dance around. My first act was to get the carbine on my side of Bud, then my left foot out of the stirrup and then calm down Bud. It takes longer to tell than it actually happened. I felt stupid hopping around, one foot in the stirrup.

"There's a good trooper. Never lost his horse," Walt drawled.

Another long wait in the warm sun made us drowsy. Finally the film crew called us for the next scene. We walked the horses up onto the road then toward the corrals. The road was icy and slippery and we let the horses pick their way past the corrals. We reached a point in the road where a secondary road intersects Highway 222. The cameras were set up at this spot for the next scene. The scene was in a small open meadow along the road with pine trees in the background. The snow was fresh and deep. We had to descend a steep embankment from the road to the meadow. I leaned back over Bud's back as we went over the side single file. We formed up in columns of two. I was on the left toward the back. I was switched toward the front with a rider who did not have a carbine. We rode through the snow at a slow trot, carbines at the ready. The camera was on the right.

"Look around and up at the cliffs. Be on the lookout for Indians," the director told us.

John and Mike were in the lead with the four Pawnee scouts. They looked good. Their heads were shaved except for mohawks down the middle. Brightly colored scarves were wrapped around their heads. Their clothing was a mixture of cavalry uniforms and Pawnee items.

We trotted past the cameras staying in file and then up onto the road. We had to find bare spots to get onto so the horses would not slip and fall. The camera crew said the shot was good and asked us to do it again.

HATZELL
SOUTH DAKOTA

It was early afternoon. We were told to unsaddle the horses and put them in the corrals for the rest of the day. Then riders were selected to ride their horses to the top of the canyon. I was not selected which was fine with me since I was on an unfamiliar horse and the ride would be up loose rock and slippery snow. The ten riders were told to get down to the Lakota village as quickly as possible, eat, and be ready to ride to the top of the canyon. They did this while we unsaddled our horses.

After taking care of the horses, we walked down to the Lakota village for lunch. It became cloudy, and a cool breeze was blowing. We began to cool down rapidly.

The Native American actors were in the village and were finishing eating as we arrived. They looked really good in their buffalo robes. I was one of the last to reach the food table. Film crew, Native American actors, and soldiers all ate from the same buffet table. Most people stood and ate. Some sat on anything that appeared comfortable enough to use. I was very tired and more thirsty than hungry. I had not had anything to drink since breakfast. As always, the food was excellent—salad, fruit, hot dishes, all kinds of meats. I found a cooler filled with juice bottles and gulped down two grape drinks. I found a dry pallet to use as a seat. It was hard to sit down with a sword and carbine strapped to you, holding a full plate of food.

Frank Costanza joined me. Frank had been very visible on the Confederate line as "Tucker". In order to be in the Search for Dunbar scene, he had to shave off his beard which he had not done for years.

After eating, I grabbed a hot cup of coffee to take away the chill. The wind was blowing strong and I picked up a few pieces of blowing trash. A U.S. Forest Service representative was there to make sure trash was not scattered about.

The ten troopers who were to go to the top of the canyon rode up the road to the Rod and Gun Campground. I poked around the teepees on the road. They looked like the real thing. A fire burned, inside one of the teepees. Native American actors and film crew members would duck inside to warm themselves by the fire.

My body and limbs began to stiffen from a combination of being out of shape, being tired, and getting cold. And then—I developed a Charlie Horse in my thumb. It curled up and shot out pain waves. I straightened it out with my other hand; but it would not stay straight.

"Rub the backside of your forearm," someone advised. In a few minutes my thumb was back to normal.

A gray-haired Native American man walked up to two young Native American men who had earlier allowed me to take their picture. They were talking in Lakota as I walked over to them.

"Hello! I just wanted to tell you guys that you look really good."

"Thanks," said one of the young men.

"Are those buffalo robes warm?"

"Yes," answered the other young man.

"Where are you from?" I asked.

"We are Lakota," answered the gray-haired man.

"Uh huh, where are you from?"

"We are Lakota," he answered again.

I'm going to have to change my side of the conversation, I thought.

"Are you from Rosebud?"

"No, Pine Ridge."

I mentioned a few people from Pine Ridge I knew whom he also knew. Jim Hatzell walked up to us.

"Mind if I take your picture?" he asked the gray-haired man.

"One hundred dollars," he answered.

"A hundred dollars?"

"That's right—one hundred dollars."

The gray-haired man did not change his serious expression. Jim could not tell if he was joking or serious.

"Can I take your picture or are you serious?" Jim asked again.

"Yes."

Jim was still uncertain. The gray-haired man finally said, "Go ahead, take my picture."

Kevin Costner was over in the largest part of the Lakota village. Several scenes were shot there. We had to stay quiet during filming.

The ten riders made it up to the western side of the canyon. We could see them on the high rocks.

There were several scenes where a Lakota man sitting on a horse on the east side of the canyon shouted something in Lakota to the people in the village. There was talk that twenty of us would have to climb to the top of the canyon and be filmed coming down the slope.

The riders on the west side were filmed and began to descend the canyon rim. They told us later the way up had been long and difficult so they decided to come down a different way. They followed a steep deer trail; but it was easier than the way they had gone up. They had to cross the swift flowing Little Spearfish Creek that reached up to the horses bellies. They crossed with no problems, rode back to the corrals, unsaddled, and took care of the horses.

Andy told us we were done for the day and to head back to the bus. At 4:00 p.m. we dropped off our carbines at the props truck on our way to the bus. We waited until the canyon rim riders joined us.

Mike Terry's friend, Spence Waldron, from Cherry Valley, New York, liked my hat.

"That's a Hardee hat isn't it?"

"Yes."

"That's the only authentic hat here. I'll buy it from you."

"No, that's okay. I like it. I formed it and I want to keep it."

"Can I see it?"

I let him try it on. He still wanted to buy it; but I said no.

Spence is in the business of providing Civil War uniforms to people. He said his were top-notch quality. He also had original uniforms that he would sell. If someone would want him to make a uniform from original cloth, he would hunt down antique cloth and make a uniform from it.

Mike Terry talked about a sacred Native American cave he had hiked to. Just as he reached the cave, a rainbow appeared, and an eagle flew under the bow which he took as a good sign.

Dean from Minnesota and I discussed farming and the environment as the bus headed back down Spearfish Canyon.

I was dead tired. John was amazed I was still functioning.

Back at the hotel, some of the guys jumped into the pool—after taking off coats and shirts. I took a good long hot shower. Liz called—everyone at home was doing well.

Andy bought beer, so we sat by the pool drinking beer and looked at each others photo albums. Fred Newcomb, still in uniform, stood in the middle of the swimming pool.

"Fred! What do you think you're doing?" someone shouted.

"I'm on rinse cycle!" he shouted back.

I was asked where we should eat supper. I suggested the Cedar House Restaurant, a favorite of my niece Erin Swift who lived in Spearfish. Wendell Anderson, Skip, Joe, John, and I piled into Skip's well-used automobile that he had bought from a rendezvouser friend for one dollar. His wife and he were in the middle of a divorce and she had taken the vehicles. We walked into the Cedar House wearing some of our movie clothes. People looked at us funny. The hostess asked us if we were with the movie and became very excited when we answered yes. The food was good and we returned to the motel.

Some of the men put on their uniforms and went to Deadwood. Deadwood was now a rip-roaring town since the state legislature had recently passed legislation to allow gambling to take place in town. We headed back to our rooms. John and I were in our beds by 9:30 p.m.

We discussed Native American religion. I told him about the Wanobi that was supposed to be a wailing sound at Crow Creek Sioux Reservation on the Missouri River. The wailing started when some artifact hunters had found an old fortified village that had existed in the 1400's. The village had been attacked and all the people killed. Their hands and feet had been cut off. The artifact hunters had started blasting away the cliffs to find human skulls to sell. That was when the Wanobi began to wail. When the destruction stopped, and the bones had been reburied, and a medicine man had performed his ceremonies, the Wanobi went away.

"It was a Bear Walker," John said. "Bear Walkers are no good. They're evil spirits." He said there are a lot of people doing pipe ceremonies and some people believe the improper use of sacred pipes can bring on the Bear Walker. He said he was actively against grave digging and had participated in several protests.

John said right before he came out for the Ft. Hays scene, the production company wanted one hundred additional arrows within two days. He stayed up that entire time making the arrows and had his family helping him. He then drove nonstop without sleep from Kentucky to the movie set. He was going to send me two Sioux arrows and two Pawnee arrows used in the movie.

John told me about a painting Richard Luce had painted for him in tribute to the 7th Cavalry at the Little Big Horn—*Spirits of the Rising Mist*. The painting is of John dressed as an Indian on one of his horses. Everything he is wearing he made. The background is the Little Big Horn. The morning mist rises and forms a large 7 for the 7th Cavalry. He said a couple years ago, the painting won the International Western Artist Award in Minneapolis. Two days after winning the award, lightning struck and killed the horse he had ridden for the picture. We came to the conclusion we were tired and we had better stop talking and go to sleep.

November 9, 1989, Thursday

The 4:15 a.m. wake-up call again came too quickly. We got up and dressed. I was not as tired as I was yesterday and not as sore as I thought I would be although my butt was aching.

The bus ride to Savoy was fairly quiet. Everyone was trying to catch a little more sleep. The air temperature felt a lot warmer than yesterday morning. We had a good hot breakfast again with plenty of coffee.

Back on the bus and then we were driven to the drop off point. We walked past the trucks and through the Lakota village where most of the teepees had already been struck. We reached the corrals and were told to get saddled up as quickly as possible. Some of the people who went to Deadwood last night were moving a little slow.

We formed up into the companies of yesterday and moved out in columns of two. I rode beside Clay Chose from North Dakota. He had been cavalry reenacting for nine years and gave me some pointers. We were to be four inches apart stirrup to stirrup and the horse in front should be four feet distant. We were traveling down the road at a fast trot. I hate trotting. The road was very slippery.

We passed through the Lakota village. The set crew was tearing down teepees and loading lodge poles onto a truck. I was surprised that none of the horses were spooked because of the way the crew was throwing the poles. Those of us who did not have carbines, stopped by the prop truck where Andy handed them to us.

Trucks and vans clogged the road. Bill Stevens passed by driving a van and waved.

Those of us towards the back of the column had to gallop at times to keep up with those in front. It was dangerous on the slippery, icy road. We passed Savoy and continued down Spearfish Canyon Road. Vertical limestone cliffs rose hundreds of feet above the spruce and aspen trees.

Now this is the way to see the Canyon, not through the windows of a car, I thought.

We reached an area where the creek had widened the valley just enough to make a small marshy meadow. Here the film crew was quickly setting up their equipment. We came to a halt and waited a long time until we were told to proceed. No one knew where we were going except for those in command. We headed down the road bank into the

meadow. It was a steep decent to the meadow. I leaned back on Bud's back. The marshy area was frozen. The horses' hooves did not break through the crust.

The lead riders came to the creek and began to cross. I had no idea how Bud would handle it. Some horses hate to cross water. The swift flowing stream reached almost to the horses' bellies. Up until my turn, all the horses crossed over with little problem.

It was now our turn. Bud hesitated and then plunged into the water up to his belly. He slowly picked his way through the forceful gurgling flow and climbed the other side with no problem. My pounding heart began to relax.

The column of horses and riders continued walking until we were up close to a grove of spruce trees. We stopped to wait for the last riders to come across Spearfish Creek.

What a great sight—the almost perpendicular limestone canyon walls, spruce and aspen trees below, the swiftly flowing stream cutting through the snow covered meadow and a line of blue-coated soldiers mounted on horses crossing the stream in double file.

Clyde's son Steve was close to the end of the column. His horse balked and refused to cross the stream no matter how much coaxing. Clyde rode back, grabbed Steve's reins, and led Steve's horse from his horse while a horse and rider on each side of Steve's horse and a horse and rider behind boxed in the recalcitrant horse. They finally pushed, pulled, and prodded him across the stream.

We continued to wait at the trees and were told we could check our gear. Mike Terry gave me a leather strap to make a carbine holder. I strapped it to the D ring for the cinch and it worked well to hold the carbine. I tightened the cinch and patted Bud to let him know I thought he was doing a great job.

We were told "Mount up!" and then "Forward march!" We headed back up the canyon angling down toward the stream until we were across from the film crew who had set up their equipment on the road.

A camp fire burned on the other side of the creek. Wayne Grace, an actor playing a major, stood by the fire with several reenactors. He said a few lines and threw his coffee on the fire. This was filmed while we rode at a trot in columns of two in the background. After the crew filmed this scene several times, we waited again.

Bill Stevens stood on the road videotaping.

The film crew brought in the big smoke machine and began generating smoke that smelled like insect repellent. The smoke drifting through the horses and riders made it look cold; but in reality the sun was warming everything up and the wool uniforms were beginning to get hot.

Kevin Costner was directing. His hair had grown long and he had a feather dangling from the back.

When the troopers in the lead saw Andy drop his arm, we would start out at a trot—head to tail, stirrup to stirrup with looks of determination on our faces. We trotted as far as we could before we would have to cross the creek. We then retraced our steps trying to stay on our past tracks. We did this scene several times.

A small depression was at the end of our trot. It rapidly turned into a muddy quagmire. It was hazardous to the horses as their hooves had broken the icy crust. Once I almost lost my seat as we trotted to a halt in the quagmire. I do not remember how many times we did this scene; but it was a lot.

We prepared to do it again, when the smoke machine ran out of gas. With that, the film crew said they had enough footage. The sound crew recorded the sounds of commands, horses' hooves, and leather creaking.

We trotted to the crossing point and crossed back over Spearfish Creek. We waited in double columns until everyone had formed up again. The film crew needed us right away, back up at the Lakota village.

We trotted almost the whole three and a half miles. I could feel my butt getting a little more sore with each bounce. We rode right on through the Lakota village without stopping.

Some of the Lakota actors frowned at us. Most smiled. One gave a mock salute. We went back to the corrals and were told to put the horses away which we did. There was very little water in the trough; but Bud did not appear to be thirsty.

We were to walk quickly back to the bus to be driven back to the Savoy camp for lunch. On the way we passed a man riding a horse and leading one of the production horses that had colic. The colicky horse laid down in the road and did not want to get up.

We reached the bus and I rode back seated beside John. We left our weapons in the bus and stood in the lunch line with the Lakota actors and film crew. Bill Stevens was in line with me and said "Once all the filming is done, I'm going to have a party to show my *Dances With Wolves* videos." Kevin was there. The meal was once again excellent. I sat across from set people who believed this movie will be of epic proportions. The temperature had been warm; but clouds rolled in and the weather was getting cooler.

We rode the bus back up the road to the Lakota village and waited a long time until several Lakota village scenes were shot. These included a Lakota man giving Dunbar a peace pipe.

We then walked up the road to the Rod and Gun Campground to wait. We had passed the four Pawnee scouts. Briggett was with them and had her picture taken with them. We got her out of the picture, got the scout who was wearing sunglasses to remove them; but could not get the one (who must be a chain-smoker) to put down his cigarette. He did hold it to the side while we took their picture. The one to the right laughed at all our cameras.

After waiting for what seemed a long time, Andy walked up to us.

"I need fifteen rough and tumble riders who can get saddled up in a hurry!" he said. He walked down the line, selecting the riders he wanted. He picked me, but did not pick any of the Nebraska people. Since Clyde was the only one who could put a bit in Bud's mouth, I asked Andy to pick someone else.

The people selected for the scene moved quickly up the road to the corrals. Bob Erickson rode up and selected sixteen of us to be filmed in the ledge scene. They had us walk up the steep slopes under the ledge. I was number ten in line to be filmed. We were to be ready and in position to fire; but did not fire. This shot would be from the waist up.

"Have looks of determination on your faces. You have tracked Dunbar for months and now have him trapped," the assistant director said before we made our climb. The climb was a hard scramble on the loose rock and snow when considering we had slick leather boots and shoes and had heavy clothing and weapons. They filmed us getting ready to fire. Kevin drove up in a jeep to watch and then took off.

The second scene was supposed to be looks of astonishment on our faces when we realize the Sioux had escaped and we had come upon an empty village. Once again this was a close-up shot from the waist up. We were to look surprised, then around to see if we could see any Sioux who might ambush us, and then look at each other in disbelief. One heavyset trooper looked goofy when he shrugged his shoulders and gave the palms up sign.

The film crew changed the position of the camera to our right and filmed us as we came down the slope. It was very difficult again because of the slick boots and loose rock and snow. We descended in one row. Clyde, several people to my right, slipped and slid down the slope on his butt. They only filmed this scene once which was unusual. The film crew said they got some great expressions on our faces.

It was a long wait as the crew filmed the fifteen riders. There was nothing special about the scene that would call for difficult riding. The group rides through a small portion of the campground and meets up with the Pawnee scouts who ride in from the opposite direction. They tell the cavalry where the Lakota camp is. This scene was filmed several different times.

A group of us brushed snow off a nearby picnic table and sat down to talk. Jack Kollodge talked to me about my journal. He said I should type it and put it on computer disk. We talked with Jim Hatzell about illustrating it, which he was interested in doing.

Bob Erickson rode up to the picnic table.

"Bob, I can't believe how close to the edge of the canyon you rode your horse. You'd never catch me that close," a rider said.

"That's nothin'," Bob answered. Onetime he had been out riding in Montana and was forty miles from where he wanted to be. A deep ravine separated him from where he needed to go. If he jumped the ravine, he would only have a ten mile ride. So he jumped it.

"I said to myself 'If I make it, I make it. If I don't, that's it,'" he said in a matter of fact tone.

After the filming of the Pawnee scouts, Andy walked over and said he needed to keep ten riders and had to let the rest go. I was one of those he let go. Most of the people he kept were those who had been cut the last day of filming at Ft. Hays. It was only fair.

The final scene of the movie was to be a wolf howling. The crew had the scene set for the wolf to howl; but he was not interested in howling. They tried everything they could think of to get the wolf to howl; but he would not do it no matter how hard they tried. John had a tape of wolf calls in his car. A crew member drove him back down the valley to get his tape then brought it back and played it on a film crew member's boom box. After hearing some of the tape, the wolf began to howl.

Filming was done for the day so we took care of the horses and walked back through what was left of the village. We turned in our carbines at the props truck and walked on toward the bus. The road had turned to mud and slush. Passing vehicles sprayed us. Bill Stevens was in the middle of a snowball fight with two film crew members.

"See you in Pierre!" he yelled dodging a snowball.

It started to drizzle. Kevin and the movie company had been fortunate with the timing of the filming for this scene.

We had a long wait on the bus. There was constant chatter. Spence Waldron had been constantly bugging me to sell him my Hardee hat.

"Spence, do you want to buy a slightly used Hardee hat?"

"Not now!"

Andy got on after everyone was loaded on the bus.

"Kevin and Tig Productions are very pleased with the filming," Andy said. He thanked us on their behalf. We would have a meeting later in the evening where he would hand out the pay checks. He would also buy a couple cases of beer. The whole bus cheered.

I was not as exhausted as I had been the last two days. When we walked into our room in the Super 8 Motel, the phone rang. It was Liz calling to see how I was.

After taking a shower, I went down to pool-side and took my photo album along. Everyone was showing each other their pictures – some were excellent. One of the Montana people passed around a large sack full of home-cured smoked deer jerky. The women from North Dakota were sitting at a table in their 1870's outfits.

Frank Costanza walked in, stripped off his clothes down to his long johns, and jumped into the pool. One of the women was taking his picture with a video camera. He pulled his pants down and mooned her.

One group of reenactors put on their uniforms and went to Deadwood to gamble. Clyde and some others headed to a bar in Rapid City. John, Skip, Joe, Paul, and I went to the Cedar House for supper. After eating, I left them and went over to Erin, my niece's house to give her a birthday present.

I returned to the Super 8 about 10:30 p.m. John was in tomorrow's scene and was already asleep. I walked down to Skip and Joe's room. The door was open, and they told me to come in. We had extensive conversations about a variety of subjects. Skip let me look at the Indian necklaces again.

Skip told us about grave witching. I had never heard of it and was skeptical. Skip said he has done it. He said it is like water witching. Hold two copper wires one in each hand straight out and they will react when over a human body. He said it will show if the body is male or female.

You can cover up a person and it will indicate their sex. In graveyards you can locate bodies and what sex they were. In one grave they got conflicting signals and discovered a baby buried at the feet of the mother. He said it really works and he does not know why.

We spent the evening telling stories, discussing uniforms, saddles, and tack. I went back to the room at midnight, being careful not to wake John since he had to get up early.

November 10, 1989, Friday

The wake up call came in at 4:30 a.m. John got up and got ready for filming. I did not go back to sleep. John went down to the lobby and brought back two coffees.

John had had some bad scrapes in his life. He was once shot in the legs by a shot gun. A tractor ran over him. His daughter had fallen in a swift stream (she was small and could not swim) he had jumped in and was able to save her farther downstream.

R.L. stopped by, he would be filming today. "Maybe we'll be working together again," he said. Paul Williams stopped in to say goodbye; he was also working today. Jim Hatzell, who was rooming with Paul, stopped in to say goodbye to John. Jim was not working. It was time for John to leave. "You can be certain there are going to be more movies," he said. We shook hands and hugged. "See you on the Custer set!" John said as he picked up his Henry and left.

Jim and I talked about his sketches and paintings. Jim said he wants to do a painting of Custer's Last Stand based on the most recent archeological information. He paints with acrylic paint since oil paints will dry out and crack. "The next time you look at a Remington, look at how much it has cracked." he said. Jim left to go back to sleep.

I took a shower, packed my things, and began loading up the Jimmy. I had not had a chance to jot down notes for this journal so I sat down and began to write until I realized I needed to take a nap.

Later, I returned to Skip and Joe's room where we continued to talk on a variety of topics. Jim came in and we talked of painting and his painting of Custer's Last Stand. "It's a rite of passage for western artists. Everyone has to attempt a Last Stand painting." and then it looked as if a light bulb had been turned on in his head. "I'm going to sketch your faces and put them in the painting!" he said. So he took the time to sketch our faces.

Clyde walked in and I paid him for the rental of Bud. He had turned out to be a good horse.

A large group of us went to the Cedar House to eat including Jack Kollodge, Buck Buxton, Dean from North Dakota, Jim, Joe, Skip, Clyde, and me. The weather was very warm.

I had not heard any news the past few days. As we were entering the Cedar House, I happened to glance at the USA Today newspaper stand. The headlines read "THE WALL IS GONE." The Germans were tearing down the Berlin Wall. I could not believe it. What a wonderful thing. Who would have thought something like this would ever happen. I can remember when President Kennedy visited Berlin and said "Ich bin ein Berliner".

We had a lively discussion about *Dances With Wolves* and the upcoming *Son of The Morning Star*. The people in the restaurant were curious about us.

Jack polled our group to see if they would be interested in a published version of the journal. They were all excited about it.

We returned to the motel where we checked out. Well, all good things come to an end and we said our good-byes. I gave Joe and Skip an old McClellan saddle to restore so I could use it in the Custer movie, *Son of the Morning Star*.

I drove east on Highway 34. The temperature was warm. I opened the window and hung out my arm. I was drowsy—it was hard to keep awake.

I had thought a lot of my Dad during the filming. He loved horses and would have enjoyed this if he were alive. If the Lord lets us see what happens on Earth after we die, I am sure he did enjoy it.

The whole movie experience was great. Each of the three experiences I had were so different I cannot say which of them I enjoyed the most. I liked them all.

CHAPTER 8 SILVER SCREEN

◆

November 18, 1990, Sunday

Huxfords and Larsons were riding with us out to Rapid City for the premiere of *Dances With Wolves*. After church and Sunday School we were on the road by 11:15 a.m. We drove out across the prairie on Highway 34 and then Highway 14 down through Philip, stopping at Wall. It was a good time, talking and speculating about what scenes would be left in the movie and what would be cut out.

We arrived in Rapid City about 1:00 p.m. The movie was to start at 2:00 p.m. The parking lot at the Rushmore Mall was already full of cars. I dropped everyone off at the main mall door so they could stand in line. I had to park very far away and walk quite a distance to reach the movie theater.

Liz was waiting. The others had gone in to save seats. A large crowd of people milled about. I saw a familiar face and shouted to Jim Hatzell. He was with Lavon Scherer from Wall, South Dakota and his wife. We found the Larsons and Huxfords and sat with them towards the front.

A large block of seats in the middle of the theater was reserved for Governor George Michelson, Senator Tom Daschle, Kevin Costner's family, and other dignitaries. I went out to the lobby to get drinks and popcorn. I talked with Francis Whitebird, State Coordinator of Indian Affairs. I saw Barry LeBeau an old friend who had worked on the movie set and talked with him. Jim and Tim had also come out to the lobby. Lakota dancers, drummers, and singers performed in the mall. We went back to our seats to wait, and what a long wait it was.

Governor Michelson and his people entered. He was eating big handfuls of popcorn. Kevin's parents sat behind him. The movie was late in starting. Everyone was nervous and wanted to get on with it.

Jim Wilson, Coproducer of the movie with Kevin, walked to the front of the theater and read a letter from Kevin. He was unable to be here because he was in England making a Robin Hood movie. He thanked the people of South Dakota. He said Roy Houck was his hero for protecting the buffalo. He would always feel a brotherhood with the Sioux people. He said he was making a film where a small group of men plot to overthrow the English king. He was not sure they would be able to do it; but if he had twenty good Sioux warriors, he knows he would be able to do it. The place went wild with whoops and clapping.

The movie finally started. It was spectacular. Most of the time, we were on the edges of our seats. I saw myself right away in the beginning playing chess in the field hospital scene, although I was far in the back and it was hard to see my face. In the battle, there was a good shot of me waving for Dunbar to ride back so we could shoot at him again. During the Ft. Hays scene, I sat at a table with four others eating. I had my back to the camera. Someone at the table says "Bill" while they are talking. Bruce saw himself cutting onions. Tim's big scene when Dunbar walks into the Headquarters building was cut out. My horse watering scene and scene where I argue with Robert Pastorelli were cut out. I can be seen out the window of the Major's office when he points to Timmons. I have my back to the camera.

After Ft. Hays, I could sit back and watch the rest of the movie in peace. It was fantastic, accurate, and beautiful.

The attack on the Lakota village was at the end of the movie. I could not see myself in the column as we set off for the Lakota village; but I did see myself in the middle of the group as we came down the slope to the village.

The movie was soon over. It did not seem like three hours—it seemed shorter. We sat through the credits and left with the crowd.

The dancers were dancing in the mall. We watched them and then went to Howard Johnson's for the reception. The place was full when we got there. All the food was South Dakota products. I had several large slices of buffalo.

Governor Michelson gave a speech. The Dream Catchers, Lakota dancers did several dances. Michael Blake the author was adopted into the White family of the Rosebud Sioux Tribe. It was an impressive ceremony. The singers and drummers called the spirits from the four corners to witness the event. They covered Blake with a star quilt. He then gave a speech and it was over.

Jim Wilson, and several of the actors signed my *Dances With Wolves* book. These people included Rodney Grant, who portrayed Wind In His Hair, Jimmy Herman, who played Stone Calf, and Floyd Red Crow Westerman who was Ten Bears. Kay Huxford was one of Michael Spears' teachers. Michael played one of the three Lakota boys who tried to steal Dunbar's horse. When Michael saw Kay he gave her a big hug.

Bill Stevens found Tim, Bruce, and me and herded us toward Tony Mangan, a reporter for the Pierre Capitol Journal who interviewed us and took our pictures.

It was a good time socializing; but it was soon time to go home. We had an uneventful trip arriving home at 11:30 p.m.

CHAPTER 9 THAT'S A WRAP

◆

The next time you view a movie, watch the people in the background. They do a great job to make the movie the best possible.

Since the making of *Dances With Wolves*, I have had the opportunity to be in four additional films. Compared to those movies, *Dances With Wolves* was the most fun. A spirit of camaraderie prevailed on the set. The major actors and film crew treated the extras as regular people.

"What have you learned?" people ask.

The main lesson was affirmation that people are basically good no matter where they are from and what their background. People genuinely want to be helpful and hospitable. This was brought home to me time and time again. During the Civil War scenes, the members of the Irish Battalion took us rookies under their wings and showed us the reenacting ropes. The Ft. Hays buckskinners invited us to sit by their fire and join in telling tales and singing along as if we had been friends for years. The Spearfish riders helped an old rusty rider get back in the saddle again.

The set buildings are slowly decaying or have been moved to more accessible locations for the public to view. Props are on display in public and private collections. In some places the scenery changes as land use changes. The video of *Dances With Wolves* can be viewed at any time; but in a way, that too is only a shadow of what really happened.

The real thing from the film is the people. Quickly forged friendships endure. Many stay in contact with each other even today—over ten year later. By the way, the Royal Order of Raccoons has continued to grow in membership. Dues are still nonexistent.

I hope there will be a sequel to *Dances With Wolves*, a reunion of friends.

About the Author

———————— ◆ ————————

Bill Markley was born on St. Patrick's Day in 1951. He and his wife Liz have been married over twenty years and have two children, Becky and Christopher. Bill is active in church and as a Boy Scout leader. He is currently the Ground Water Quality Program Administrator for the South Dakota Department of Environment and Natural Resources. He is responsible for a variety of environmental protection and cleanup programs. While on annual leave from his job, Bill had the good fortune to be an extra in five movies including: *Dances With Wolves, Son of the Morning Star, Far and Away, Gettysburg*, and *Crazy Horse*. He was a member of an Antarctic research team for two expeditions in 1972 and 1973 in the Dry Valleys of Antarctica. As a boy he worked on the family farm in Pennsylvania taking care of cattle, horses, and other animals as well as general farm work. He has a BS degree in Biology and an MS degree in Environmental Science and Engineering from Virginia Polytechnic Institute and State University. His favorite hobbies include: writing, reading, Civil War infantry and frontier cavalry reenacting, hiking, and camping. Bill has lived in Fairview Village, Pennsylvania for17 years, Blacksburg, Virginia for 6 years, and Pierre, South Dakota for 24 years. He has kayaked and backpacked in Alaska, traveled to Hawaii, the Bahamas, Canada, Antarctica, New Zealand, Fiji, the Kingdom of Tonga, and spent a week on the Pacific Ocean traveling from Tonga to New

Zealand aboard a Tongan banana boat. Bill has kept journals through most of his experiences, possibly material for future books.

About the Illustrator

◆

Jim Hatzell, originally from Chicago, Illinois, is a graduate of the American Academy of Art. In addition to a career in fine art and photography, Jim has worked in show business since appearing in the motion picture *Dances with Wolves*. He has also performed equestrian work in the films *Son of the Morning Star, Far and Away, Gettysburg, Geronimo—an American Legend, Lonesome Dove II, Buffalo Girls, Buffalo Soldiers, The Postman, Two for Texas*, and *Ride with the Devil*. He has worked behind the scenes in production in *Lakota Woman* as Re-Enactor Coordinator (also 1st speaking role), set dressing for *Wyatt Earp*, featured actor in *Crazy Horse* as Curtis the reporter, and also trained extras in how to march, drill and soldier for *Rough Riders*. He has worked in wardrobe, set design, extra hiring, wrangler, and technical advisor, in addition to various duties in a large number of documentaries, music videos, & commercials. Jim has resided in Rapid City, South Dakota since1981. He established Fiddlers' Green Studio in 1988. He enjoys the mediums of acrylic, watercolor, and Pen-N-Ink. He is also an accomplished cartoonist with a specialty in caricature. More of Jim's work can be viewed at his web site http://artistride.dtgnet.com. To contact him please call: (605) 341-0620 email: fiddlersgreen@dtgnet.com